People and Profits?

The Search for a Link Between a Company's
Social and Financial Performance

3 Day

LEA's Organization and Management Series
Arthur Brief and James P. Walsh, Series Editors

People and Profits?

The Search for a Link Between a Company's Social and Financial Performance

Joshua Daniel Margolis
Harvard University

James Patrick Walsh
University of Michigan

2001

LAWRENCE ERLBAUM ASSOCIATES, PUBLISHERS
Mahwah, New Jersey
London

Lawrence Erlbaum Associates, Inc., Publishers
10 Industrial Avenue
Mahwah, NJ 07430

Cover art by Pamela Martel Bernstein

Library of Congress Cataloging-in-Publication Data

Margolis, Joshua Daniel.
 People and profits? : the search for a link between a company's social and financial performance / Joshua Daniel Margolis, James Patrick Walsh.
  p. cm. — (LEA's organization and management series)
  Includes bibliographical references.
 ISBN 0-8058-4011-7 (paper : alk. paper)
 1. Social responsibility of business. 2. Corporations—Finance. 3. Profit.
  I. Walsh, James Patrick, 1953– . II. Title. III. Series
 HD60 .M365 2001
 658.4´08 —dc21
                                                            2001016168
                                                                  CIP

Books published by Lawrence Erlbaum Associates are printed on acid-free paper, and their bindings are chosen for strength and durability.

The final camera copy for this work was prepared by the author, and therefore the publisher takes no responsibility for consistency or correctness of typographical style. However, this arrangement helps to make publication of this kind of scholarship possible.

Printed in the United States of America
10 9 8 7 6 5 4 3 2 1

Table of Contents

Acknowledgments

Our interest and work in this project has been sustained by a number of institutions and individuals. We would like to thank the Aspen Institute Initiative for Social Innovation through Business for its financial support of this project. More important, we want to thank Judith Samuelson, the Institute's director, and Mary Gentile, a consultant to the Institute, for their unflagging interest, deep insight, and personal commitment to this project. The University of Michigan Business School added its financial support to this project as well. Recognizing that this topic area is defined by a host of important questions that all defy easy answers, Dean B. Joseph White has been a staunch supporter of this work. We appreciate his encouragement and enthusiasm for the project. Seminar participants at Columbia University, Harvard University, University of Michigan, University of North Carolina, and Yale University provided constructive feedback and new leads as we were developing and refining our work. A lively group of scholars and practitioners attending a seminar at the 1999 Business for Social Responsibility annual meeting helped to articulate the need for this effort.

Finally, we could not have completed this project without the incredibly able work of our research assistants. Nichole Pelak, Marguerite R. Booker and Seung-Yoon Rhee worked tirelessly as bibliometric sleuths, spending the better part of a wonderful summer cloistered in the library tracking down many of these research papers. Jeffrey Lang took over for them after we had gone through the papers and carefully checked our work with a fine-tooth comb. Research librarian Joann Sokkar helped us find even the hard-to-get articles and answered all questions that arose along the way. Chet Miller gave us careful and insightful feedback on our "final" draft. And finally, Pam Bernstein and John Zagorski worked their computer magic at the end to pull the entire effort together.

Thank you all.

Boston and Ann Arbor
September, 2000

About the Authors

Joshua Daniel Margolis is an Assistant Professor of Business Administration at the Harvard Business School. Prior to joining the Harvard faculty he was a Fellow in the Society of Scholars at the University of Michigan. He received his BA from Yale University and his MA and PhD from Harvard University. Joshua's research focuses on organizational ethics, integrating philosophical and social scientific approaches to questions of business and professional ethics.

James Patrick Walsh is the Gerald and Esther Carey Professor of Business Administration at the University of Michigan Business School. A Fellow of the Academy of Management, he received his BA from the State University of New York at Albany, MA degrees from Columbia University and from the University of Chicago, and his PhD from Northwestern University. Basic questions about the purposes and accountability of the contemporary firm orient Jim's current research interests.

Series Editor's Foreword

Arthur P. Brief
Tulane University

LEA's Organization and Management Series was launched with the intent of providing a home for book-length scholarly works that were likely to shape the future of our field of inquiry. Joshua Margolis and Jim Walsh, my co-editor, have written a book that more than admirably achieves this objective. I am absolutely confident that scholars concerned with the social-financial performance relationship will turn to the book for guidance. This is so because it provides a comprehensive review, critique, and integration of the empirical literature that truly enlightens. But, this book accomplishes much more, for it is not just about organizational effectiveness conceived of in sterile dollars and sense terms. It is about community, charity, the environment, and human rights. Corporate social performance captures a dimension of organizational effectiveness that is alive, that goes beyond merely increasing wealth to a concern for sharing it with those less fortunate. Joshua and Jim have produced a book that makes a reader feel this humanness. It makes me super proud that it is in our Series, independent of its evident scholarship.

People and Profits?

Section 1: Introduction

What is the relationship between the social performance of companies and their financial performance? More colloquially, can a firm effectively attend to both people and profits as it conducts its business? This question has been investigated in no fewer than 95 empirical studies published since 1972. We have assembled a compendium of this research to give researchers and practitioners alike a broad overview of these 95 studies and a systematic database detailing the content of each one.

Empirical inquiry into the relationship between companies' social and financial performance – between their concern for humanity and their concern for the bottom line – has received ongoing attention since Bragdon and Marlin published the first empirical study in 1972, with 21 studies completed in the 1970s, 32 in the 1980s, and 42 in the 1990s (see Figure 1). In the most recent five-year period from 1996 through 2000, researchers published 31 new studies, and no doubt more are set to follow. Figure 1 also reveals the years in which the firms' social initiatives under investigation actually occurred. Of course, it is in the nature of the research process to see a lag between the year of publication and the year of empirical observation. It is no surprise to discover that studies published in the 1970s investigated firms' activities in the 1960s. The empirical focus on firm activity has generally kept pace with the times.

Our aim here is to provide a comprehensive portrait of this research literature. We suspect that policy makers and executives alike will appreciate having this work crisply summarized. The tables and figures that accompany section three offer a quick and easy overview of what academic research has been saying over the last 30 years. The research community should find it helpful as scholars work to craft new theory, ask novel questions, and conduct even more sophisticated empirical investigations. The detailed accounting of all 95 studies in Exhibit 1 provides a foundation from which scholarly work can continue.

Our portrait of this work begins, in section two, with a broad orientation to the literature, exploring why the link between social and financial performance has been subject to continual inquiry and often heated debate. In section three, we present an integrated overview of the 95 studies. Through a series of tables and figures, we illuminate the nature of the studies conducted; the data samples selected for investigation; the ways in which financial and social performance have been measured; and the overall tally of results. Section three includes a table distilling the conclusions drawn and directions proposed in twelve previous reviews of the academic literature. Following the tables and figures, an exhibit outlines each of the 95 studies, providing a detailed view of the literature and a basis for systematic comparison. This compendium concludes with a comprehensive bibliography, organized to highlight the 95 studies themselves, as well as the work that provided much of the theoretical and methodological background to this line of inquiry. An appendix explains abbreviations and acronyms used throughout this document.

Section 2: A Brief Orientation to the Question

2.1 Constructing the Business Case for Corporate Social Performance

In an effort to justify and advance – or to delegitimize and jettison – the activities that fall under the umbrella of social performance,[1] researchers and managers alike want to understand the relationship between corporate social performance and corporate financial performance. A positive connection between social and financial performance establishes a business case for having firms pursue activities motivated by societal needs and concerns.[2] If these activities can be shown to contribute to improved financial performance, the underlying logic goes, then companies themselves benefit from adopting practices designed to help a variety of constituents.

A business case may help justify a company's involvement in social initiatives, but the search for a link between social and financial performance begs a fundamental question. Why are firms called upon to engage in social initiatives in the first place?[3] We propose two intertwining explanations: (1) social trends drive a recurring reconsideration of the role and responsibilities of the firm, altering what is expected of corporate entities; (2) firms find themselves in situations that call upon them to respond, independent of any systematic reconsideration of a firm's purpose and responsibilities.

First, the role of the firm is continually questioned with each successive wave of dawning social awareness in larger U.S. society. Pollution in the 1970s, South African apartheid in the 1980s, and international human rights abuses in the 1990s are emblematic of issues that instigated social movements. Efforts to redress these wrongs implicated company practices, calling into question the means through which companies generated their profit. The specific issues themselves required responses from companies, pushing executives and managers to consider the social impact of their profit-making endeavors. But pollution, apartheid, and human rights abuses have also raised broader questions about the role and responsibilities of the firm within society. These specific issues, among others, made evident the intimate relationship between corporate practices and social concerns. As a result, companies have increasingly been called upon to solve problems to which they have contributed, such as pollution, as well as those for which, though not causally responsible, they are potential beneficiaries or even uninvolved bystanders.

Companies have had to consider their social performance for a second reason. Companies continually find themselves in new situations, undertaking a broader range of activities. It is not simply a matter of having the role of the firm reassessed under the weight of rising social concerns, but rather, an ever-shifting role emerges from the reality of taking on new responsibilities. With globalization, firms operate in regions where the basic institutions of Western welfare capitalism simply do not exist. In order to operate, firms must perform the functions that government might otherwise be expected to perform.[4] Meanwhile, in the United States, and in some other industrialized nations, the tremendous success of corporations since the 1970s, and the economic prosperity they have produced, are juxtaposed to the limitations and perceived failings of other societal institutions, particularly those of government. As a result, companies are asked to extend their effectiveness and step in – for educational programs, volunteer drives, and public health initiatives, to name a few examples – where other institutions might formerly have been counted upon.

The reality of having to do new things dovetails with an ongoing reconsideration of the purview of the firm, together drawing companies into civic activities. At its root, the forces drawing companies into social performance rest on the conviction that the engines of tremendous economic growth might be able to expand what they do to improve the lot of humanity, beyond the contribution they make to economic growth.[5] However, from the perspective of owners, executives, and managers trying to generate financial returns from a set of assets, the logic that makes the firm a target for moral and social appeals, and the forces that draw corporations into social initiatives, says nothing about the impact these activities have upon the firm itself. A business case documenting financial gains from social performance can hasten efforts to gain corporate involvement, allay fears about its costs to the bottom line, and provide a rhetorical cudgel for proponents and rhetorical cover for executives.

2.2 Academic Debate

The practical reality of corporate social initiatives and attempts either to justify or invalidate them has motivated researchers to investigate the connection between corporate social performance (CSP) and financial performance (FP). In addition, inquiry into the relationship between corporate social performance and financial performance contributes to hoary debate about vying theories of the firm (Berle, 1931; Dodd, 1932; Orts, 1993; Bradley, Schipani, Sundaram and Walsh, 1999). Proponents of a narrow economic role for the firm may point to negative and neutral financial returns from social performance, and to a connection between antecedent financial performance and subsequent social performance, as evidence that socially responsible practices squander a firm's (and thus shareholders') resources. Proponents of a broader role for the firm may point to positive and neutral financial returns from social performance as evidence that an expanded set of responsibilities neither jeopardizes the financial role of the firm nor squanders resources.

Empirical evidence of a positive causal relationship moving from social performance to financial performance also promises, for some, a solution to endless debate about the

4

role and responsibilities of the firm. If social performance turns out to contribute to financial performance, competing models of the firm might converge. The need to return once more to first principles about the "true" purpose and nature of the firm would disappear, as a broad conception of the firm's role and responsibilities might be perfectly consistent with a narrower conception. Those who construe a narrow economic role for the firm would embrace a financial rationale for socially responsible practices, and those with a broader conception of the firm's responsibilities would need not appeal to an alternative construal of the firm's purpose to justify expansive responsibilities. Demonstrating the bottom-line benefits of corporate social performance would make room for humanitarian concerns within the paradigm of shareholder wealth-maximization. For those debating the theory of the firm, there is much at stake, and thus great academic interest, in identifying the relationship between social and financial performance.

Independent of any debate about the purpose and purview of the firm, understanding the determinants of financial performance is a central interest for all research focused on business.[6] A company's financial performance is a function of innumerable variables. Isolating the effect that a firm's socially responsible practices have on financial performance contributes to the broader program of tracing financial performance to a variety of factors and their interrelationships.

2.3 Purpose of this Compendium

Within the context of continuing corporate initiatives, demands for even greater corporate involvement, and lively academic debate and inquiry, this research compendium is designed to achieve three aims. We seek to (1) provide a comprehensive portrait of academic research into the relationship between social and financial performance; (2) to create a template for reviewing this literature, from which future research and theory can build; and (3) to lay the groundwork for engaging *different* questions,[7] questions implicated but often unexamined in the quest to document a relationship between social and financial performance.

Section 3: An Integrated Portrait of the Empirical Literature

3.1 Method

This compendium covers empirical studies that examine the link between socially responsible conduct -- positive acts of corporate social performance -- and financial performance.[8] To identify studies for this compendium, we followed the process outlined by Capon, Farley and Hoenig (1990) in their review of work on the determinants of financial performance. We began by searching the computerized database ABI/Inform and the references listed in prior review articles on corporate social performance. From the articles collected, we repeated the process, culling additional citations from references until no new studies were found. In addition, suggested articles and chapters were generated at interim presentations of this work at five different academic institutions in winter 1999 and spring 2000 and at the 1999 Business for Social Responsibility conference.

To be included in the compendium, a study had to meet several criteria: (1) be published or accepted for publication; (2) contain at least one variable the authors specified to be measuring the financial performance of companies, and at least one variable the authors specified to be measuring the social performance of companies; (3) report the relationship between the measures of social performance and financial performance. Studies examining the relationship between irresponsible corporate actions and financial performance were excluded, as were studies where inferences could not be drawn about the corporation as the unit of analysis. In total, we reviewed 95 studies published in 94 articles and books.

Each article was read three times (once each by the two authors and once by a research assistant) and coded in two different ways. The tables and figures were produced through a joint coding process performed by the authors in tandem. The database of studies that appears in Exhibit 1 below was assembled in a sequential process, with the authors alternating responsibility for entering the information in a computer file and editing it. A research assistant then validated the information by checking each entry against the original article.

Although all 95 studies report results about the link between social performance and financial performance, the articles are divided into four broad categories: 86 specifically about performance; 4 about disclosure; 3 about reputation; and 2 miscellaneous. Exhibit 1 uses these categories to ease interpretation. It is important to note that nine of the 95 studies make evidence available about the relationship between social and financial performance, though they are not designed explicitly to test that relationship. The other 86 studies explicitly report tests of the relationship between social and financial performance. These nine studies are specifically identified in the bibliography.

3.2 Corporate Samples

Over half of the 95 studies examine exemplary, notorious, or very large firms. Figure 2 shows the distribution of these 56 studies, which sample on what might be considered to be good, bad, and big companies. The single most common sample of companies used by researchers to examine the relationship between social and financial performance is *Fortune* magazine's database of corporate reputations. The annual survey conducted by *Fortune* ranks the most admired American corporations by asking executives, outside directors, and corporate analysts to evaluate the companies they admire most on eight attributes.[9] Milton Moskowitz, an editor of *Business and Society Review*, put together his own list of exemplary companies in the early 1970s, a list that has been used by others as well.

The path-breaking work of the Council on Economic Priorities (CEP) in the late 1960s and 1970s made data available on the environmental records of companies in highly polluting industries.[10] Researchers have drawn heavily on the CEP sample of firms and have also assembled their own sample of firms in the notoriously "dirty" chemical, oil, pulp and paper, steel, and textile industries.

In addition to saints and sinners, researchers have tended to focus on large firms, drawing samples from popular lists of the largest corporations. The *Fortune* 500 and 1250, Standard & Poor's 500, *Forbes* 500s, and the *Business Week* 1000 have all been used by researchers.[11]

3.3 Measuring Financial Performance

In the 95 studies covered, financial performance is measured in 70 different ways (see Table 1): 49 accounting measures, 12 market measures, 5 measures that mix accounting and market indicators, and 4 other measures of outcome performance. The two dominant methods used to measure financial performance in these studies reflect different time horizons. Accounting measures are taken to be indicators of past performance, and market measures are taken to reflect future performance. Of the 49 accounting measures, eleven focus on risk and fourteen measure return. The return measures can be subdivided into three categories: six variants of return on equity (ROE), four variants of return on assets (ROA), and four variants of return on sales (ROS). Of the 11 market measures, three focus on risk and seven focus on return

3.4 *Measuring Social Performance*

Theorists have gradually developed a comprehensive definition of corporate social performance (Wood, 1991),[12] but even with a comprehensive definition in hand, measuring social performance has remained elusive. The 95 empirical studies reviewed here draw on 27 different data sources to assess social performance (Figure 3) and cover 11 different domains of corporate practices (Figure 4). Some scholars applaud the multiple methods and measures used to assess corporate social performance (Gephart, 1991; Simerly, 1999), arguing that the polyglot properly reflects the diversity of corporate practices that constitute social performance. Recurring calls have also gone out, however, to develop a set of common measures that are valid and reliable (Ruf, Muralidhar and Paul, 1998; Spicer, 1978; Wokutch and McKinney, 1991).

To grasp the many ways that social performance has been measured, consider the eight major categories into which the 27 data sources are grouped in Figure 3: multidimensional screening criteria, surveys, conduct in South Africa, organizational programs and practices, disclosure, money spent, environment, and reputation. These sources of data roughly correspond to the domains of corporate practices that researchers investigate when studying corporate social performance (Figure 4). Environmental practices are the most commonly measured aspect of social performance. Not far behind, we see omnibus measures, such as the *Fortune* reputation ranking, which asks respondents for a global assessment of a firm's social responsibility, and the Kinder, Lydenberg, Domini (KLD) index, which explicitly evaluates multiple dimensions of companies' social performance.

Two prominent examples, spanning the period in which most of the 95 studies have been conducted, illustrate the expanse of what constitutes corporate social performance, both in practice and in empirical research. In 1975, Milton Moskowitz (1975: 29), a prominent advocate for corporate social responsibility, listed the following set of criteria for identifying stellar and poor social performers:

> Pollution control, equal employment opportunity, minority and female representation on the board of directors, support of minority enterprise, responsible and irresponsible advertising, charitable contributions, community relations, product quality, plant safety, illegal politicking, disclosure of information, employee benefits, respect for privacy, support for cultural programs, responsiveness to consumer complaints, fair dealings with customers.

The second indicative example of how social performance has been measured is the KLD database. Two of the more recent studies included in this compendium (Berman, Wicks, Kotha, and Jones, 1999; Waddock and Graves, 1997) draw on the KLD rating criteria as a measure of social performance. Both studies go to great lengths to explain the rating system. KLD rates companies on five criteria, along a scale of –2 to +2, depending upon the extent to which companies engage in practices manifesting poor social performance (called "areas of concern") and good social performance (called "areas of strength"). These five criteria are community, diversity (formerly referred to as "treatment of women and minorities"), employee relations, natural environment, and product safety and quality.[13] Two other KLD criteria are binary negative screens. The presence of either of these reduces a company's social performance rating: involvement in nuclear power and involvement in weapons-related military contracts. A third negative screen, equity holdings in or revenues from South African operations, has been dropped from the current KLD ratings but has been used historically in many studies that draw on the KLD ratings.

3.5 Summary of Results

Corporate social performance is treated as an independent variable, taken to predict or causally precede financial performance, in 80 of the 95 studies. In these studies, the majority of results (53%) point to a positive relationship between corporate social performance and financial performance (see Figure 5). The conclusion often drawn from these results is the classic notion that firms do well by doing good: social initiatives contribute to the bottom line.

Corporate social performance is treated as a dependent variable, taken to be predicted by or causally preceded by financial performance, in 19 of the 95 studies. In these studies, the majority of results (68%) point to a positive relationship between corporate financial performance and social performance.[14] The conclusion often drawn from these studies is that firms that make money have the ability to devote resources to social initiatives.

When treated as an independent variable, corporate social performance is found to have a positive relationship to financial performance in 42 studies (53%); no relationship in 19 studies (24%); a negative relationship in 4 studies (5%); and a mixed relationship in 15 studies (19%).[15] The studies reporting mixed results include seven that report both a positive relationship and no relationship; five that report a positive relationship, a negative relationship, and no relationship; one that reports both a positive and negative relationship; and one that reports both no relationship and a negative relationship. One study reporting mixed results finds a U-shaped relationship (Bowman and Haire, 1975), with intermediate levels of corporate social performance associated with the highest levels of financial performance.

When treated as a dependent variable, corporate social performance is found to have a positive relationship to financial performance in 13 studies (68%); no relationship in 3 studies (16%); and a mixed relationship in 3 studies (16%).[16] The studies reporting mixed results include two that report a positive relationship, negative relationship, and no relationship between social performance and financial performance, as well as one study reporting both a positive and negative relationship.

The results can be illustrated further by sorting them according to a variety of criteria. We can picture them by the year of publication (Figures 6 and 7), sample type (Figures 8 and 9), data source (Figures 10 and 11), domain of investigation (Figures 12 and 13), type of analysis (Figures 14 and 15), and whether or not the researchers used a time-lag to examine the CSP-FP relationship (Figure 16). Although it may be tempting to draw inferences from the seemingly consistent patterns of results in these various figures, these consistent results may reflect two very different realities. Such consistency may be a sign of a reliable and stable result, but it may also reflect uncontrolled and systematic bias.

3.6 Mechanisms and Control Variables

The findings might be encouraging for advocates of corporate social performance and problematic in the eyes of opponents and critics, but they certainly illuminate the path for further research. First, what begs investigation is the causal mechanism that would link social performance and financial performance. Second, future research must consider the role of social performance alongside other factors that contribute to corporate financial performance.

A central challenge for researchers is to unearth the mechanisms that causally connect social and financial performance. The existing literature tends to implicate two broad

11

causal mechanisms, one positive and one negative. On the one hand, social initiatives enable companies to capture additional benefits from stakeholders, benefits that drop to the bottom line. Morale among employees and trust within the local community, both of which may result from corporate social performance, enable the firm to operate more effectively and efficiently. Reducing pollution may cut operating costs; adhering to environmental standards may be a spur to innovation.[17] In addition, by addressing the concerns of multiple stakeholders, managers signal their skill and ability to the capital markets, which some argue enhances the value of the firm.[18] On the negative side, corporate social performance reduces the likelihood of costly sanctions. Taking care of customers and the community, as well as the environment, for example, reduces the likelihood of lawsuits, government penalties, and public disapproval. Avoiding these costs, again some argue, makes a firm more attractive to shareholders.

Any model that purports to explain a firm's financial performance must also attend to the range of factors that contribute to it. Therefore, researchers investigating the contribution of social performance must control for a host of other antecedent factors. Scholars have indeed included a wide variety of control variables (see Table 2), but their multiplicity and seemingly *ad hoc* nature makes it very difficult to compare results across studies. As a consequence, it is nearly impossible to identify the relative contribution that social performance makes to financial performance. A systematic and theory-based selection of other institutional, industry, and firm level factors would help to identify the magnitude of this discrete contribution.

Although industry effects, company size, and market risk are three of the most widely included control variables, 19 studies include no control variables at all. Ten of those 19 treat social performance as the independent variable and find a positive relationship with financial performance. The findings in those ten studies suggest that CSP contributes to FP. By omitting control variables, though, the studies leave open the possibility that the relationship observed between social and financial performance may be spurious and, indeed, a product of a factor left out of the analysis. Concerns along these lines introduce deeper questions about the data and statistical analyses that lie behind the research findings covered here. Improvements in both data and analyses would advance research into the link between social and financial performance.

3.7 Conclusions

The clear signal that emerges from thirty years of academic research -- indicating that a positive relationship exists between social performance and financial performance[19] – must be treated with caution. Serious methodological concerns have been raised about many of the studies and about efforts to aggregate these results (Arlow and Gannon, 1982; Griffin and Mahon, 1997; Roman, Hayibor and Agle, 1999; Wokutch and McKinney, 1992; Margolis and Walsh, 2000). Questions arise about the connection between the underlying CSP construct and efforts to measure it; the validity of the measures used to assess social performance; the diversity of measures used to assess financial performance; and the direction and mechanisms of causation, given the heavy reliance on correlation analyses and contemporaneous financial and social performance data. The questions, criticisms, and recommendations voiced in past reviews of this research are distilled in Table 3.[20]

It is worth wondering where continued research into this question will take us. Is the financial impact – positive, negative, or neutral – of corporate social performance necessary or sufficient either to support or to invalidate the involvement of firms in the range of activities classified as social performance? There may well be sound reasons to have firms involved in certain socially responsible practices, even if there are steep and unrecoverable costs to the firm.[21] Similarly, significant financial gains that accrue from socially responsible practices may not outweigh other reasons that argue against those practices.[22]

For advocates and opponents of corporate social performance alike, research and practice may both be enhanced if we stepped back from the quest for a missing link. Evidence of an association between social and financial performance may promise to settle theoretical disputes over the purpose and responsibilities of the firm, and it may provide rhetorical artillery for those seeking to advance corporate efforts. But the search for that evidence may well cause researchers to neglect other crucial questions, questions that may be equally pressing. From the perspective of managers and executives, it seems especially important to understand how best to manage corporate social initiatives. From the perspective of larger society, it seems especially important to consider the conditions under which society is well served by corporate solutions to social problems.[23]

End Notes

[1] The variety of activities that constitute social performance are described below. For a broad conceptualization of social performance and its components, see Wood, 1991. For simplicity, we use "social initiatives," "social performance," "socially responsible practices/activities," and "civic activities" interchangeably.

[2] The assumption that the financial impact of social performance should determine the legitimacy and continued existence of corporate social initiatives is subject to critical scrutiny. Whether or not the financial impact turns out to be positive, neutral, or negative, it may be the case that other considerations are as important, or even more important, in determining whether companies should be involved in these social initiatives. We expose this entire line of inquiry to critical scrutiny and explore the many questions raised by the search for a link between social and financial performance in our paper, "Misery loves companies: Whither social initiatives by business?" (Margolis and Walsh, 2000). However, in the present book, we focus on describing past research.

[3] The search for a link between social and financial performance begs the question, in fact, of why firms are engaged in social initiatives. That is an empirical question others have examined in the past (Austin, 1998; Tichy, McGill and St. Clair, 1997; Teoh and Thong, 1984), and a question we are currently investigating in a survey of a stratified random sample of 540 companies. Empirical research can help us develop a coherent theory of why and how companies come to get involved in these activities. There remains the question taken up here, however, of why *companies* in particular, as an institutional set, have been called upon to engage in these activities.

[4] In addition, pressures arise from the first source as well. Companies operate amid societies where the welfare of local inhabitants, whether in the form of wages, education, or basic rights, invokes a reassessment of the role of the firm beyond its profit-maximizing objectives.

[5] According to World Bank estimates, of all developing regions of the world, only South Asia and China enjoy sufficient economic growth to halve poverty by 2015 (World Development Indicators CD-ROM, 1999). That still leaves more than half the people in five other regions of the world in poverty: East Asia and the Pacific; Europe and Central Asia; Latin America and the Caribbean; Middle East and North Africa; and Sub-Saharan Africa. If contributing to economic growth is the most direct benefit to human welfare that companies provide, as significant as that is, then figures such as those from the World Bank help explain why more is often sought from companies. This is not to minimize the importance of companies' economic impact on human welfare and development, and it should be seriously considered whether extending firms' activities puts that economic contribution in jeopardy. But when the economic gains are placed in the larger context of human welfare, it makes sense at least to ask what else companies might do on behalf of society, or how they might operate to advance human welfare on multiple fronts.

[6] See Capon, Farley and Hoenig (1990) for a review of 320 studies examining the determinants of financial performance.

[7] We introduce a variety of questions and considerations raised by research into corporate social performance and suggest a complementary agenda for practice-driven research and theory in our own work (Margolis and Walsh, 2000).

[8] For a review of studies examining the relationship between corporate social irresponsibility and financial performance, see Frooman, 1997.

[9] The advantages, disadvantages, cautions, and caveats associated with using the *Fortune* reputation database have been debated extensively by Brown and Perry (1994, 1995), Fombrun and Shanley (1990), Fryxell and Wang (1994), Simerly (1999), and Szwajkowski and Figlewicz (1997).

[10] Eleven of the studies included for review in this publication use CEP data. Seven of the eleven use only the CEP reports on environmental performance, issued in the 1970s and covering firms in highly polluting industries. The four other studies use the CEP database expanded in the 1980s to cover multiple domains of social performance. Only the six studies that use the actual CEP sample focusing on pollution control are included in Figure 2. One additional study uses the same data but on a sub-sample, and another looks at pollution control as one of eleven criteria – neither are included in Figure 2.

[11] The *Forbes* 500s from 1981 (May 11, 1981, volume 127, number 10) were used by Aupperle, Carroll, and Hatfield (1985). *Forbes* ranked the 500 largest companies in each of four different dimensions: sales, assets, profits, and market value. The total number of companies that year, across all four lists, was 818.

[12] Wood (1991: 693) defines corporate social performance as "a business organization's configuration of principles of social responsibility, processes of social responsiveness, and policies, programs, and observable outcomes as they relate to the firm's societal relationships." Within this tripartite definition of social performance, Wood goes on to specify three principles of social responsibility, three processes of social responsiveness, and three socially relevant sets of policies, programs, and outcomes.

[13] These five criteria are the most commonly used in research using KLD data. However, KLD has recently added two additional criteria: "other," which captures issues pertaining to governance, and "international operations," which evaluates a company's outsourcing and suppliers. See Waddock, Graves, and Gorski (2000) for further discussion.

[14] Five studies investigate the relationship in both directions, which explains why there are more results than studies.

[15] These figures are rounded to the nearest full percentage point, and so, sum to 101% in this instance.

[16] These figures are rounded to the nearest full percentage point.

[17] For a thorough review of evidence about the impact of environmental regulation on competitiveness, see Jaffe, Peterson, Portney and Stavins, 1995.

[18] For a theoretical examination of why firms may attend to stakeholders, see Donaldson and Preston, 1995, and Narver, 1971.

[19] As striking, perhaps, as the majority of results that indicate a positive relationship is the limited number of negative findings. Even when the findings contained within studies reporting mixed results are included, only 12 reveal any negative relationship between social performance and financial performance.

[20] While six years passed from the publication of the first empirical study to the first review, eleven reviews were published in the ensuing twenty-two years. Seven reviews have been published in the past ten years alone (eight, if you count this book). We believe that this quickening pace of scholarly activity reflects the increasingly urgent need to reconcile wealth creation and human welfare.

[21] Of course, it would be intriguing to investigate how firms might reduce the costs they incur for these sorts of programs without diminishing the benefit enjoyed by the beneficiaries of the programs.

[22] Tetlock (2000) recently investigated the effect of managers' philosophies of human nature on their decision making (including their attitude toward various corporate governance perspectives). He noted that we do not yet know if disagreements rooted in value difference might be as easy to resolve as disagreements rooted in competing views of the facts of the situation. He was skeptical. Indeed, he observed that "Academics who rely on evidence-based appeals to change minds when the disagreements are rooted in values may be wasting everyone's time" (p. 323).

[23] The importance of these questions and others are discussed more extensively in our paper (Margolis and Walsh, 2000).

Table 1
Measures and Use of Financial Performance Indicators in the Corporate Social Performance Literature

Accounting Measures	# of studies where used
Return	
ROE	
ROI	31
Operating Ratio (on equity)	7
ROC	1
ROIC	1
Cash-basis ROE	1
ROA	
Cash-basis ROA	28
ROA (IBSGLT/A)	1
Operating Ratio (on total assets)	1
ROS	
Sales Growth	13
Operating Ratio (on sales)	8
Operating Leverage	2
Risk	
Debt/Equity	6
Current Ratio	4
Debt/Assets	3
EBIT/Interest Expense	2
Altman's Z	1
Capital Expenditures/LT Debt	1
Debt Coverage	1
Liquidity	1
Quick Ratio	1
Std Dev of ROIC	1
Variance of EBIT/Average EBIT	1

Accounting Measures	# of studies where used
Other	
Total Assets	3
Operating Income Growth	3
Asset Growth	2
Asset Turnover	2
Assets	2
Capital Intensifies	2
Earnings Growth	2
EPS	2
EPS Growth	2
Post-tax Income	2
Sales	2
Dividend Growth	2
Net Income	2
Asset Age	1
Change in Cash Flow	1
Change in Dividend Amount	1
Equity	1
Employee Growth Rate	1
Log of Sales	1
Operating Income	1
Before-tax Profit	1
Savings per Dollar Spent	1
(debt+market value of equity-assets)/sales	1
Rating relative to industry	1

Market Measures	# of studies where used
Return	
CAR	7
Alpha	8
Total Return	6
Mean Abnormal Returns	6
Risk Adjusted Return	4
Monthly Average Return	2
Other Abnormal Returns	1
Market Risk	
Beta	8
Std Dev of Total Return	3
Residual Error	1
Other	
Stock Price	2
Share Price Growth	2
Mixed Market & Accounting	
Price/Earnings	7
Market to Book Value	3
Dividend Yield	3
Excess Value	2
Tobin's q	1
Other Performance Measures	
Operations (Efficiency)	4
Market Share	3
Perceptions of Value	1
Mutual Fund Purchases	1

Table 2
Control Variables and the Number of Studies Using Each

Control Variable	N	Control Variable	N	Control Variable	N
none	19				
industry	41	industry growth rate	1	number of other firms in SMSA	1
size	32	change in sales	1	government spending	1
risk	13	asset turnover	1	federal income tax/pre-tax income	1
leverage (debt/equity)	7	operating environment	1	tithing club in area	1
advertising intensity	7	strategy	1	age of company	1
industry concentration	4	initial net income	1	managers or individuals owning 5%+ of company	1
R&D intensity	4	capital intensity	1	PAC contributions	1
firm growth rate	3	dividend payout ratio	1	size of corporate public affairs staff	1
asset age	3	growth in real wages	1	sponsor of philanthropic foundation	1
acid-test ratio	2	spectrum diversity	1	outside directors	1
managerial control of firm	2	propensity to acquire	1	institutional ownership	1
CEO compensation	2	price to cost margin	1	timing of regulations	1
past financial performance	2	cost of labor	1	time	1
overall market performance	2	GDP growth	1	award giver	1
sales growth	1	multinationality	1	previous awards	1
comparison period	1			investment in manufacturing	1

Table 3
A Review of the Reviews

Authors	Number of Studies Reviewed	Appraisal of the Literature	Suggested New Directions
Aldag and Bartol (1978)	10	• Social responsibility is a nebulous concept • Operationalizations are suspect • Causality is not established • Discrepant findings	• De-emphasize the term and focus on socially relevant activities in the areas of OT, OB, QWL, values, and equal employment • Longitudinal studies • Experimental designs
Arlow and Gannon (1982)	7	• Different measure of social responsibility and economic performance assessed over different time periods confound comparisons • Social responsibility measures have dubious validity • Focus on common stock returns ignores such factors as the state of the economy	• Study lagged relationships

Cochran and Wood (1984)	14	• Measures of CSR are not wholly adequate
		  – Reputation indices are highly subjective and limited to small samples
		  – Content analyses focus on idiosyncratic variables; moreover, do firms do what they say?
		• Measures of FP have serious defects:
		  – Investor returns: often no controls for dividends, risk, and industry
		  – Accounting returns: influenced by growth rates and firms' accounting practices; control for leverage and risk
		• Samples and control groups are too small
		• Time periods are too short
			• Better measures or CSR are desperately needed (use perceptions of more extensive activities)
			• Explore additional explanatory variables (asset age)
			• Causality should be investigated
			• Event studies

Authors	Number of Studies Reviewed	Appraisal of the Literature	Suggested New Directions
Aupperle, Carroll and Hatfield (1985)	10	• Concepts are value laden and subject to ideological and emotional interpretations • Difficult to develop valid measures of CSR • Little effort to empirically test definitions, propositions and concepts • Researchers tend to create their own measures rather than build upon past work	• Go beyond reputation surveys and content analyses to assess CSR • Examine whether or not the CEO's orientation to CSR is shared throughout the firm • Employ measures of FP that are not susceptible to corporate manipulation; moreover, control for risk and time • Be prepared for equivocal results: "Perhaps this issue, whether or not corporate social responsibility is related to profitability, will never be completely resolved"
Ullmann (1985)	13	• Conceptualizations and operationalizations of key terms are problematic • Content analysis and reputational indices vary in level of refinement and sophistication • Models of financial disclosure may not apply to social disclosure • Other influences and intervening variables are not taken into account	• Need new ideas and approaches for measuring social performance • Longitudinal studies • Control for executive values, company size and visibility, strategic posture, past/current economic performance, industry, risk, stakeholder power, mandated vs. voluntary social initiatives

Authors	Number of Studies Reviewed	Appraisal of the Literature	Suggested New Directions

Wokutch and McKinney (1991)	20	• Little consensus on the exact meaning of CSP
		• Researchers have yet to design meaningful, multidimensional models of CSP:
		  – Perceptual measures - raters may be uninformed, lack of inter-rater reliability, time and context dependent
		  – Content analyses - firms have motives to under- and over-report CSP activities
		  – Proxy behavioral measures - a single dimension of a multi-dimensional construct that is industry-specific and not necessarily "objective"
		• Unsettled questions concerning the appropriate measures for FP:
		  – Accounting-based measures - differing and incompatible time frames, differing measures susceptible to changing accounting practices and executive control, the past may not predict the future
		  – Market-based measures - may reflect information unrelated to a firm's social responsibility or profitability
			• Employ multiple methods and levels of analysis to assess CSP (perceptual and behavioral measures, interviews, archival data, participant observation)
			• Employ both accounting and market measures of performance
			• Examine CSP in an international context

Wood and Jones (1995)	34	• The CSP construct is not well-specified • The simplistic connection between social and financial performance has never received a serious challenge in the literature – The direction of causality between CSP and FP, if any is even implied in the work, is rarely clear • The great variety of CSP measures makes it difficult to aggregate the reported research results. • The literature confuses which stakeholders are represented by which measures of corporate social performance… and their associated effects	• The expectations, effects and evaluations of CSP activities need to be better matched to the stakeholders involved in these activities

22

Authors	Number of Studies Reviewed	Appraisal of the Literature	Suggested New Directions
Pava and Krausz (1996)	21	• Uncertainty surrounding the definition of CSR • CSR variables may not be completely valid • Empirical tests have not been well-designed…yet no systematic biases are evident • Most studies rely on observation of CSR activities prior to 1975 • However, "methodological diversity should mitigate problems associated with experimental deficiencies which might result from any one approach"	• Update earlier studies • Examine the role of the CEO in establishing CSR goals • Examine how corporations defend and justify their CSR expenditures in their annual reports
Griffin and Mahon (1997)	51	• Academics and practitioners alike should be concerned with the variability and inconsistency in the reported results • Continued focus on large, cross-sectional, inter-industry studies mask individual and industry-specific manifestations of CSP and FP • Perceptual measures of CSP may be biased by erroneous information or attention to what a company says it does, over what it does do • A unidimensional index of a multidimensional construct is problematic • It is difficult to develop validity and reliability checks for FP measures when 70% of them have been used only once	• Measure actual CSP, not perceptions of it • Conduct single industry studies • Focus on a few key CSP and FP measures to improve internal validity • Learn why and how firms persist with CSP activities despite disappointing FP

Preston and O'Bannon (1997)	8	• The connection between corporate social and financial performance has not been fully established
		  – Direction – are CSP and FP positively or negatively associated, or not at all?
		  – Causality – does CSP produce FP or vice-versa, or is there a synergistic relationship between the two?
		• Inevitable problems of measurement
			• Specify the theory and test it

Authors	Number of Studies Reviewed	Appraisal of the Literature	Suggested New Directions
Richardson, Welker and Hutchinson (1999)	14	• A failure to model the process that links CSP to FP • Samples chosen to maximize the likelihood of finding or rejecting hypothesized relationships • Degree of information redundancy among the three sources used to measure CSP (company disclosures, reputation indices, direct data on limited aspects of CSP) has not been thoroughly investigated • Bias in the literature toward environmental performance (admittedly because these data are available) • Research on linkage between CSP and the capital markets has been poorly designed	• Need strong theoretical underpinnings and refined experimental designs • Event studies on specific CSP investments and expenses • Interdisciplinary work • Control for industry • Maintain visibility of the CSR issue in the scholarly literature
Roman, Hayibor and Agle (1999)	37*	• Reclassified 26 of 62 results in the Griffin and Mahon (1994) review, correcting the overly negative view of the relationship between CSP and FP • It is time to admit the methodological shortcomings of much of the work in this area; treat this flawed work as an argument, not as evidence	• Define the multidimensional CSP construct and then obtain reliable and valid measures of it

*An additional nine studies in the review examined corporate social irresponsibility.

24

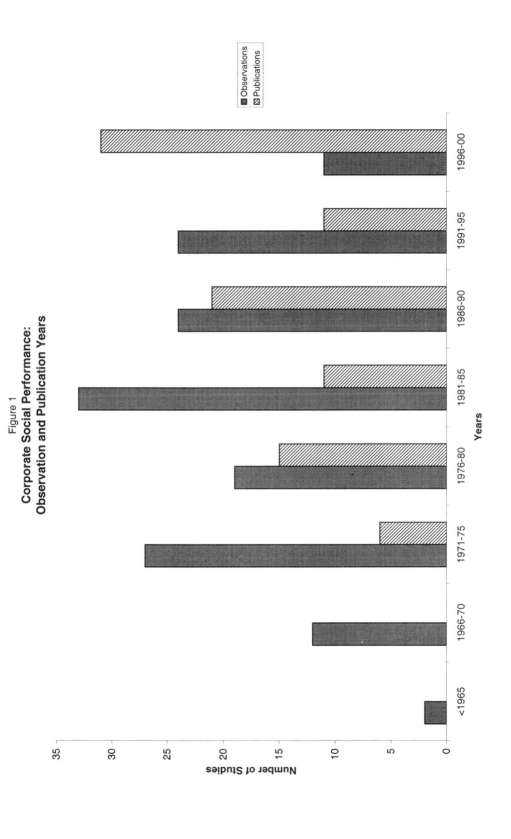

Figure 1
Corporate Social Performance:
Observation and Publication Years

Figure 2
Corporate Social Performance:
Sampling on the Good, the Bad, and the Big
in 56 of 95 Studies

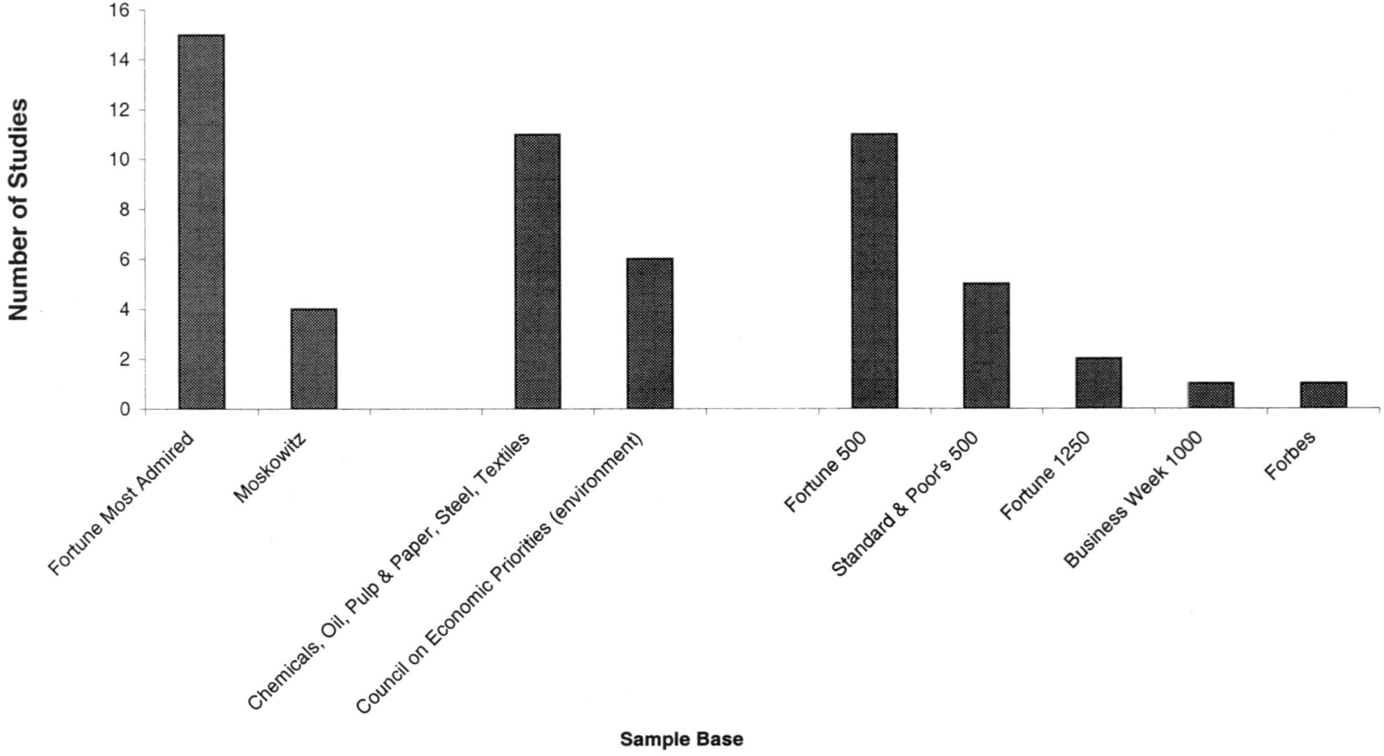

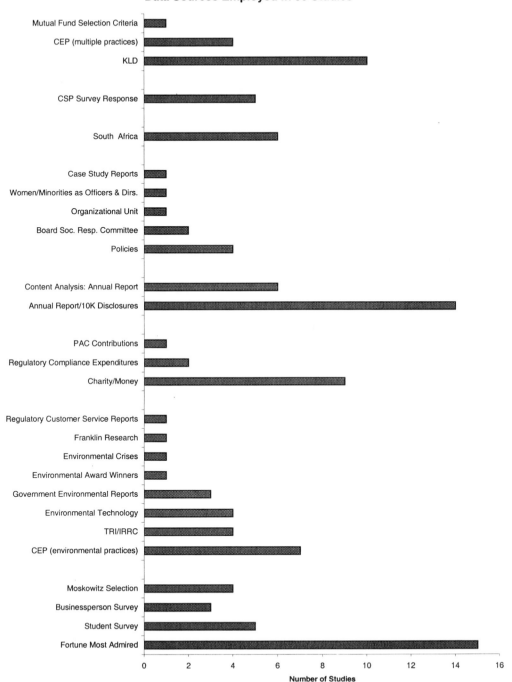

Figure 3
**Measuring Corporate Social Performance:
Data Sources Employed in 95 Studies**

Figure 4
Corporate Social Performance:
Domains of Investigation in 95 Studies

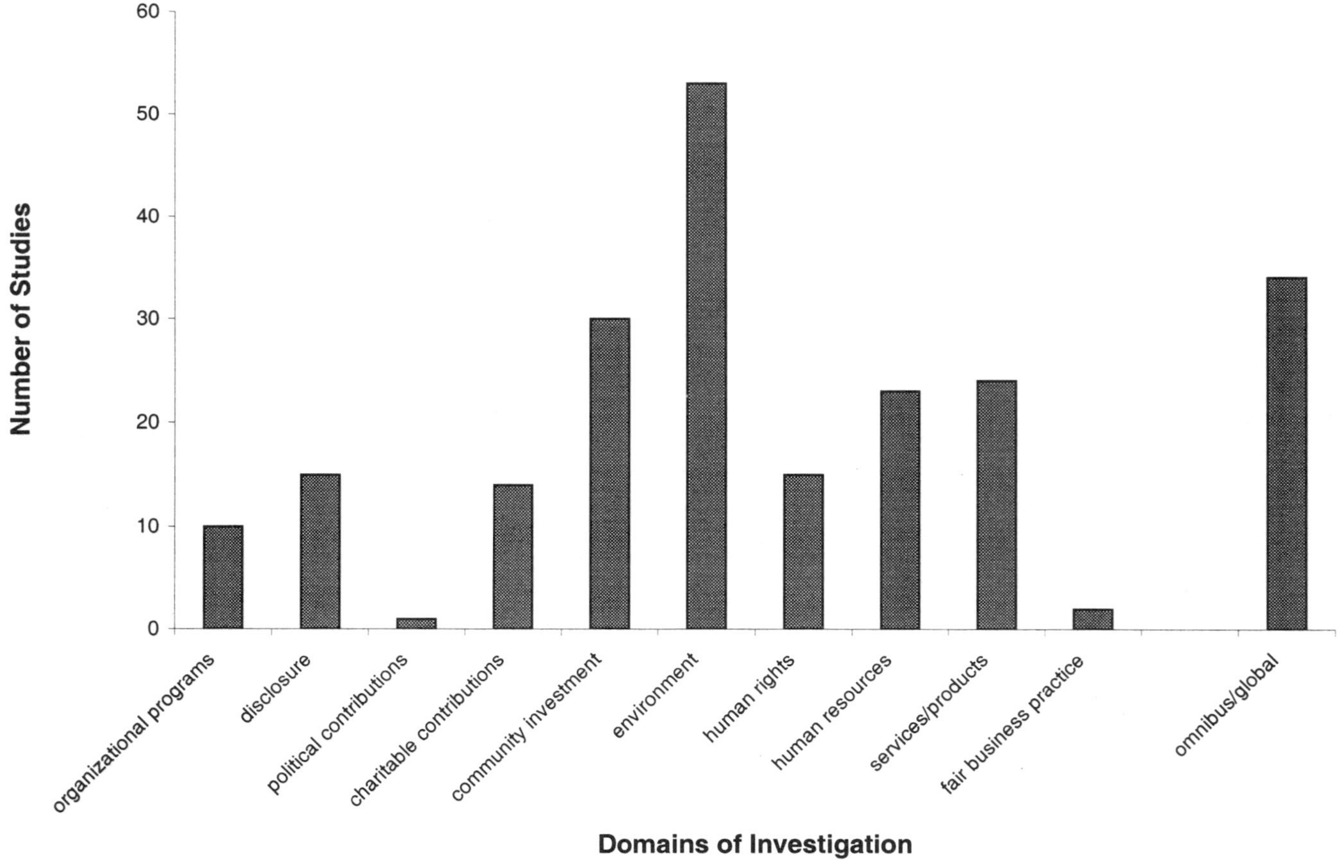

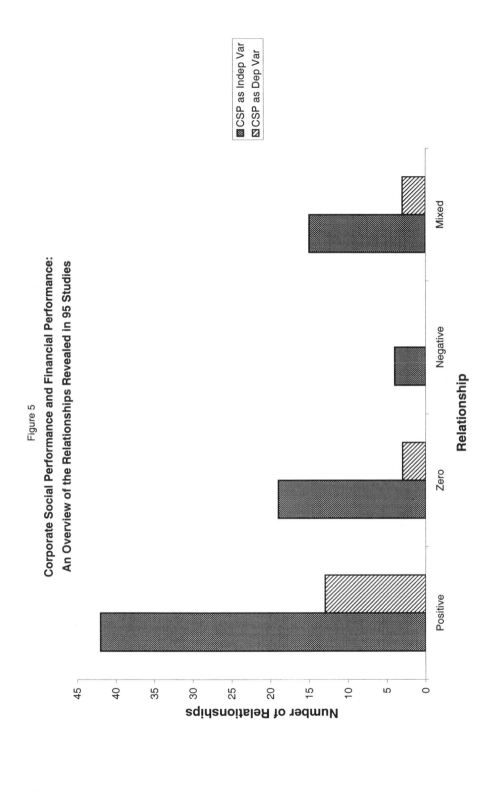

Figure 5

Corporate Social Performance and Financial Performance:
An Overview of the Relationships Revealed in 95 Studies

Figure 6
Results by Year of Publication:
Corporate Social Performance as Independent Variable

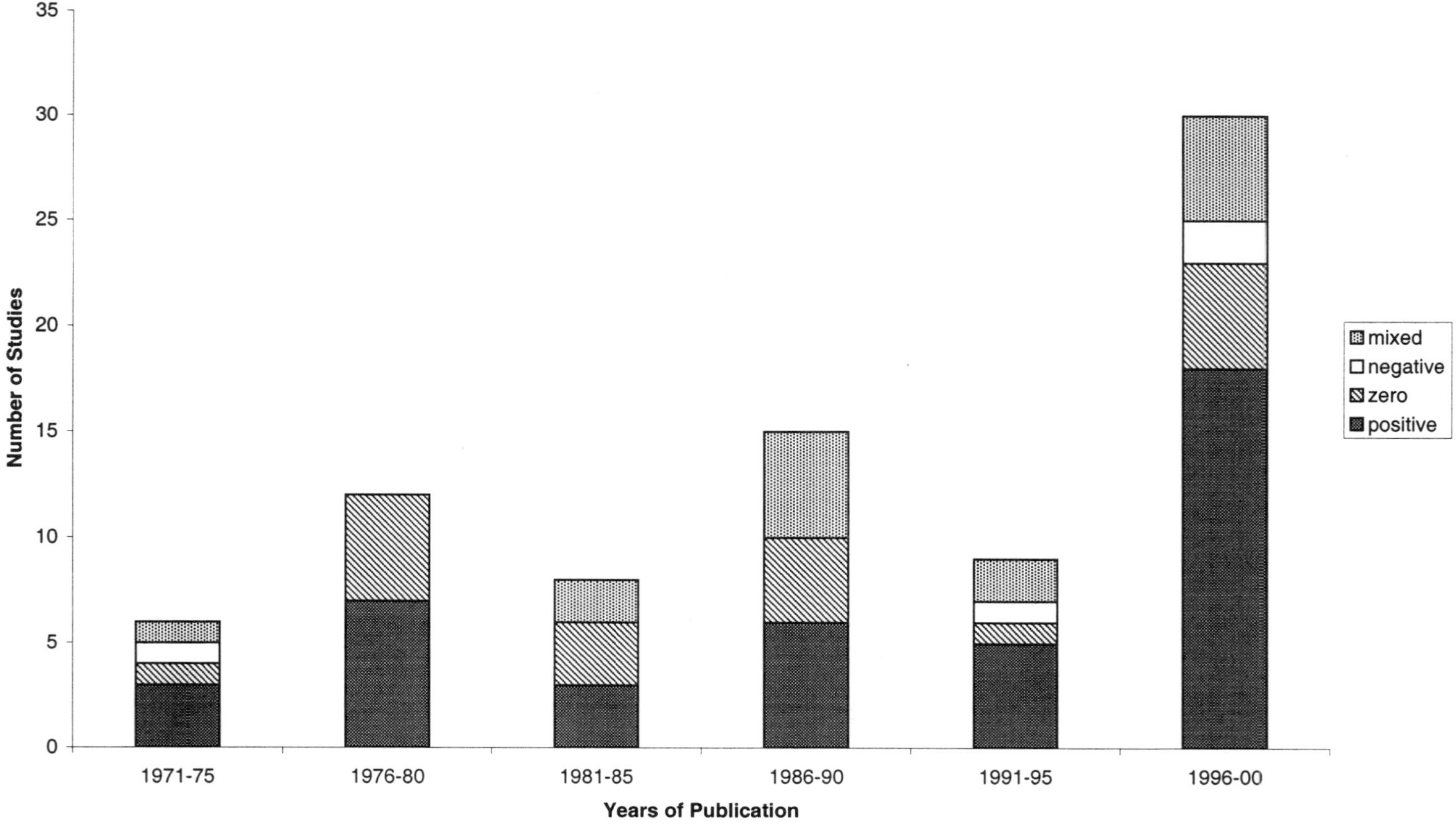

Figure 7
Results by Year of Publication:
Corporate Social Performance as Dependent Variable

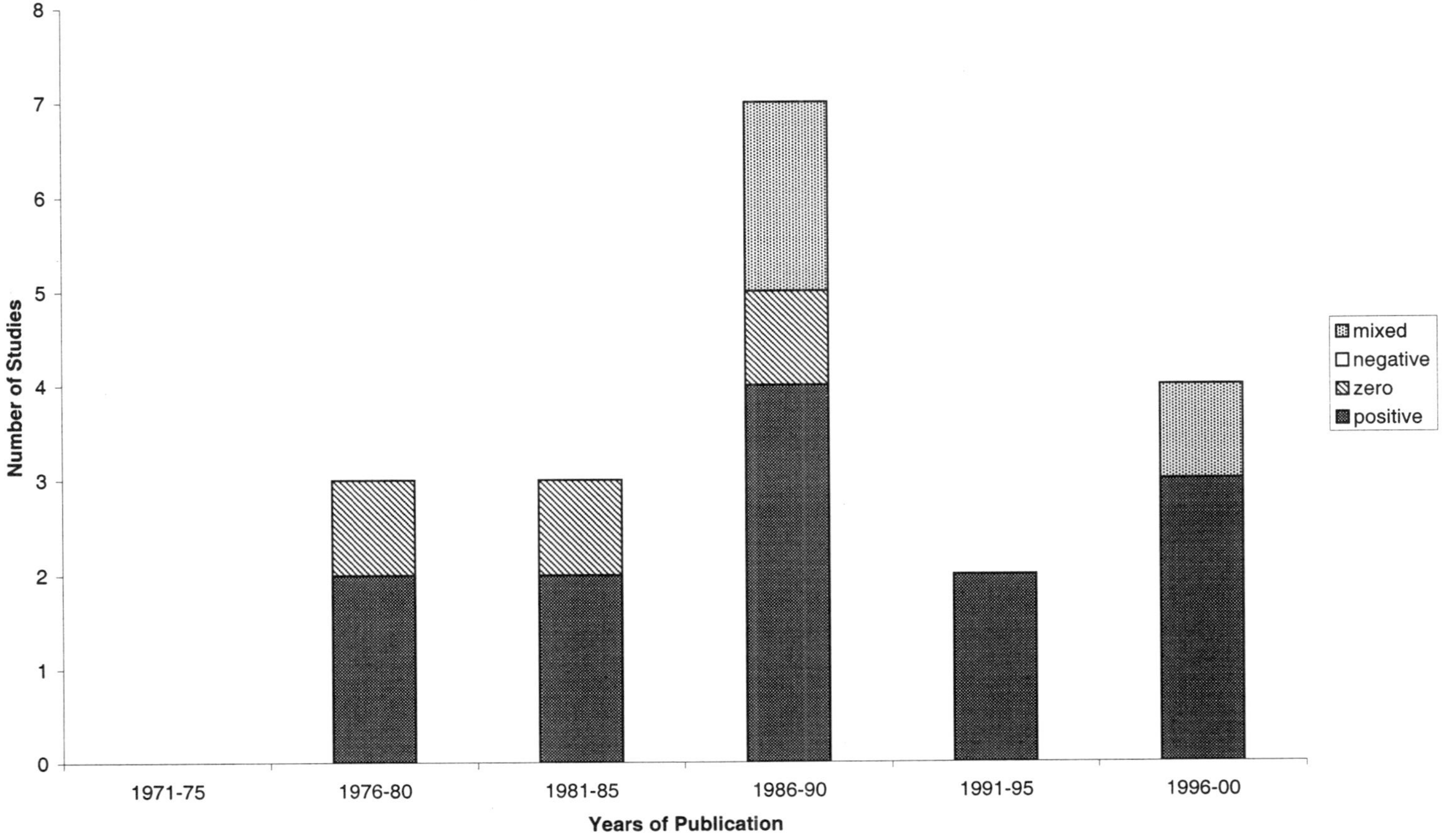

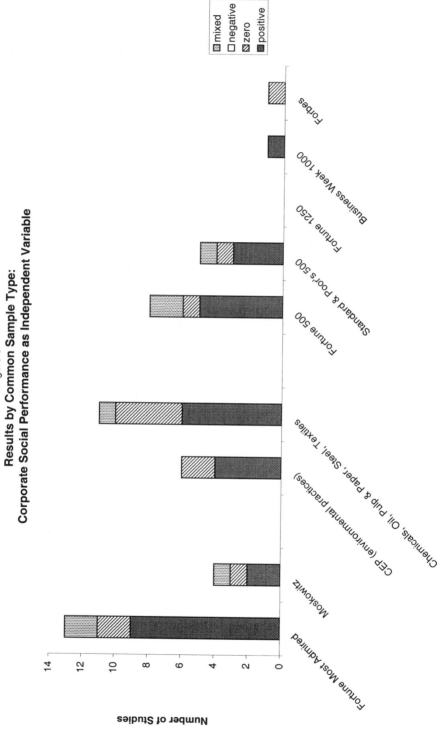

Figure 8
Results by Common Sample Type:
Corporate Social Performance as Independent Variable

Figure 9
Results by Common Sample Type:
Corporate Social Performance as Dependent Variable

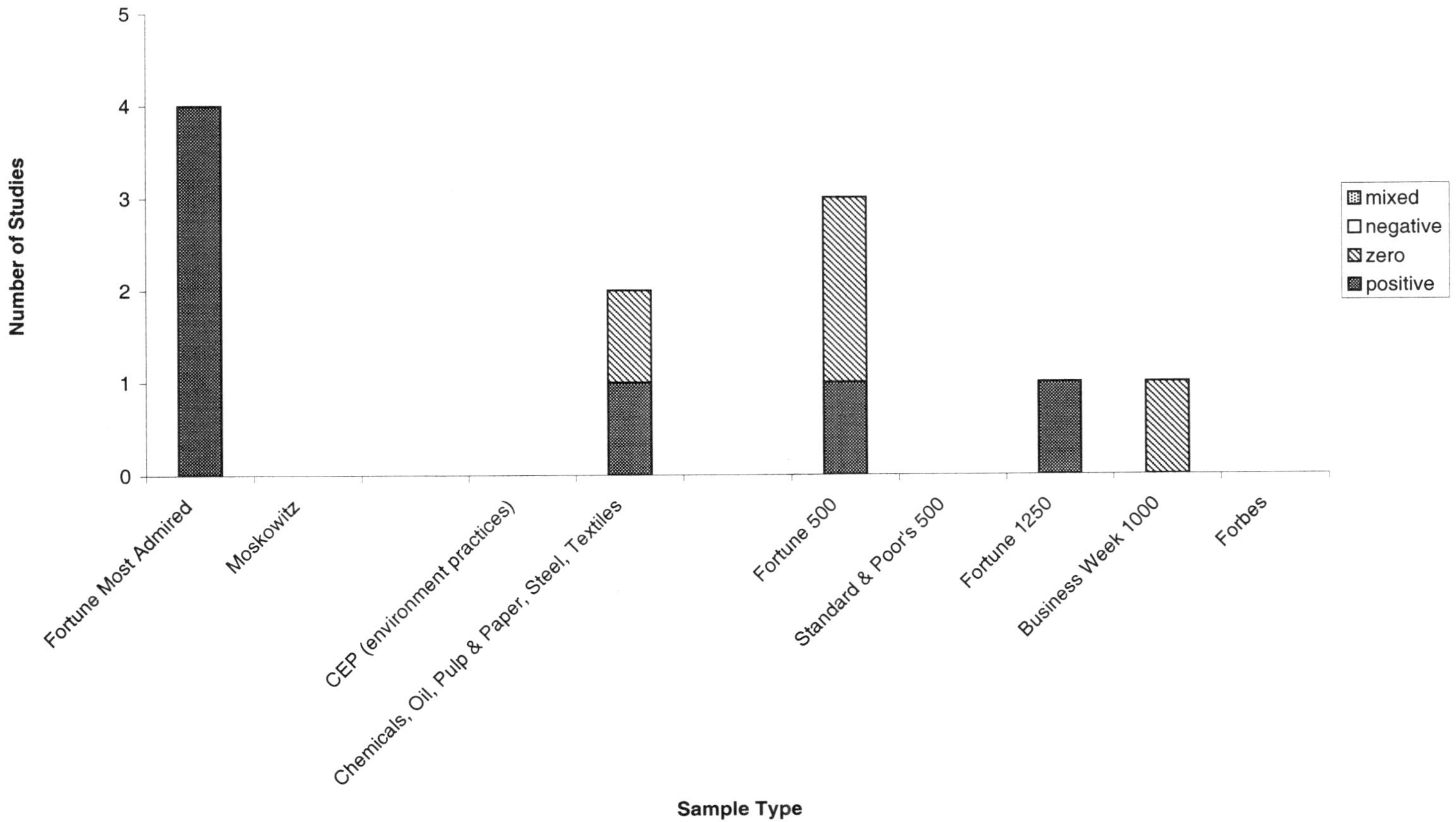

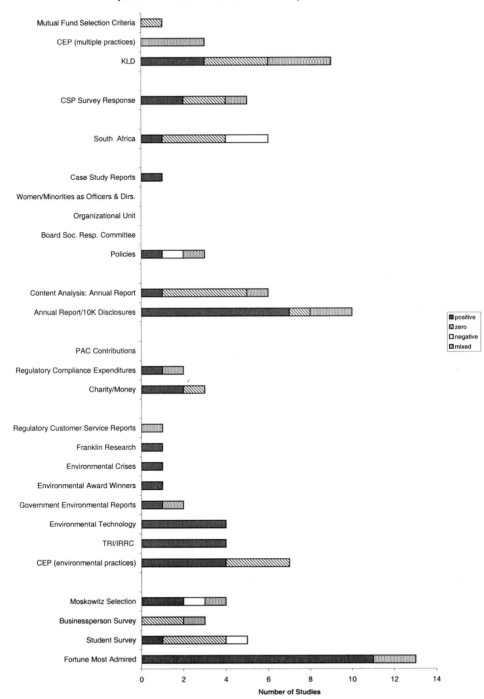

Figure 10
Results by Data Source:
Corporate Social Performance as Independent Variable

Figure 11
Results by Data Source:
Corporate Social Performance as Dependent Variable

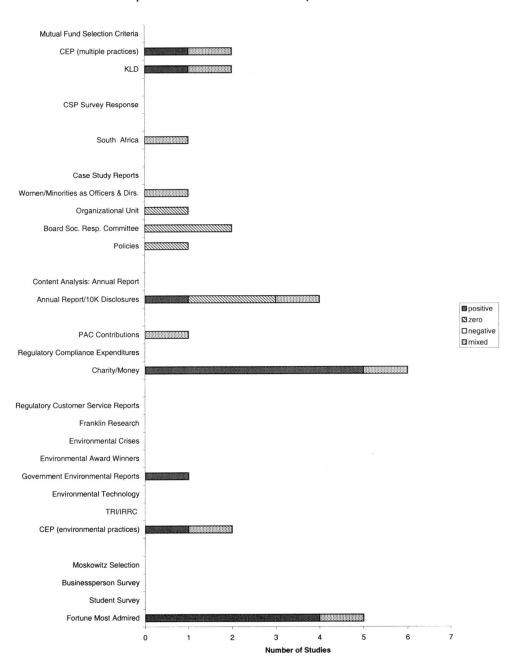

Figure 12
Results by Domain of Investigation:
Corporate Social Performance as Independent Variable

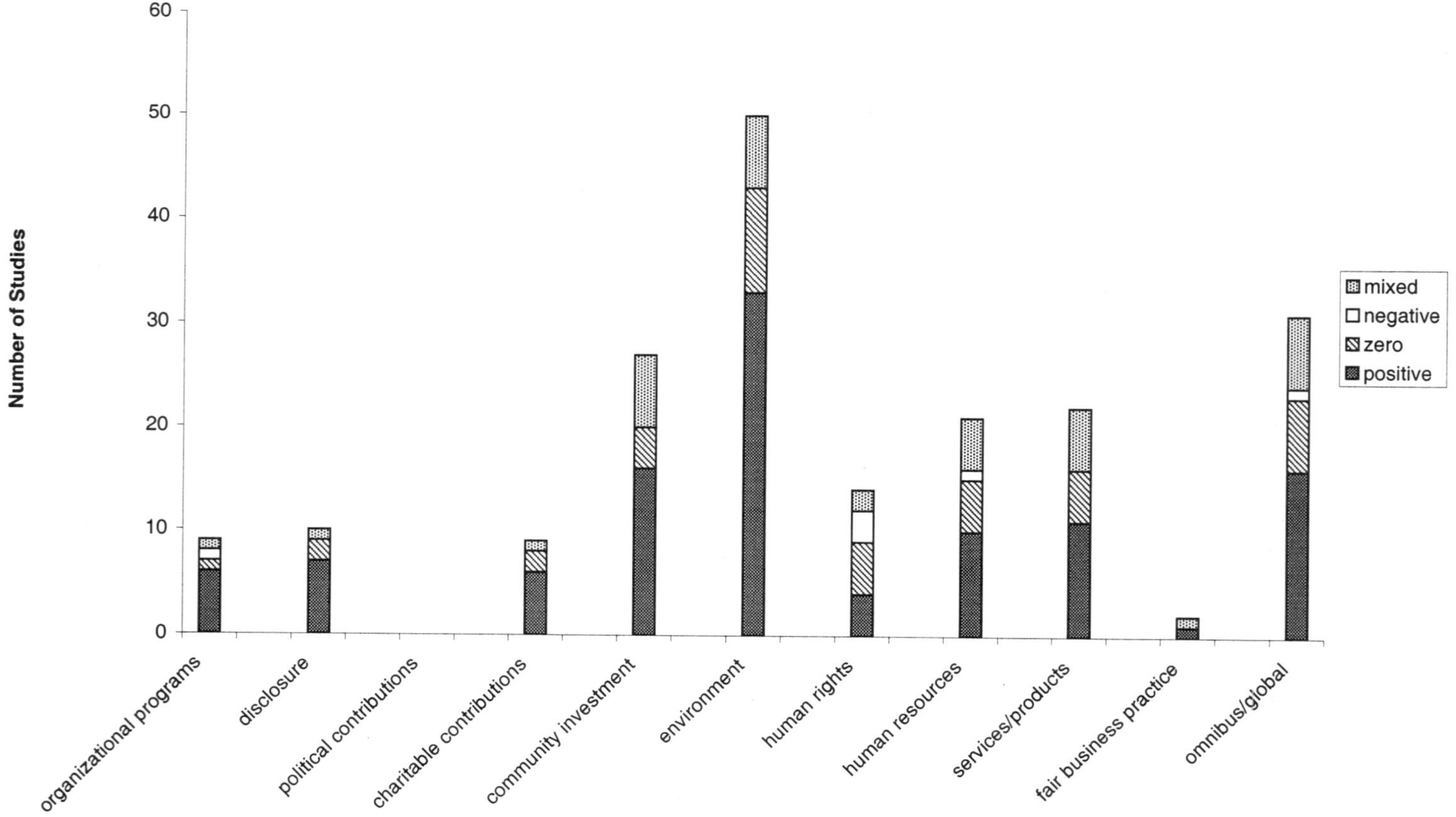

Figure 13
Results by Domain of Investigation:
Corporate Social Performance as Dependent Variable

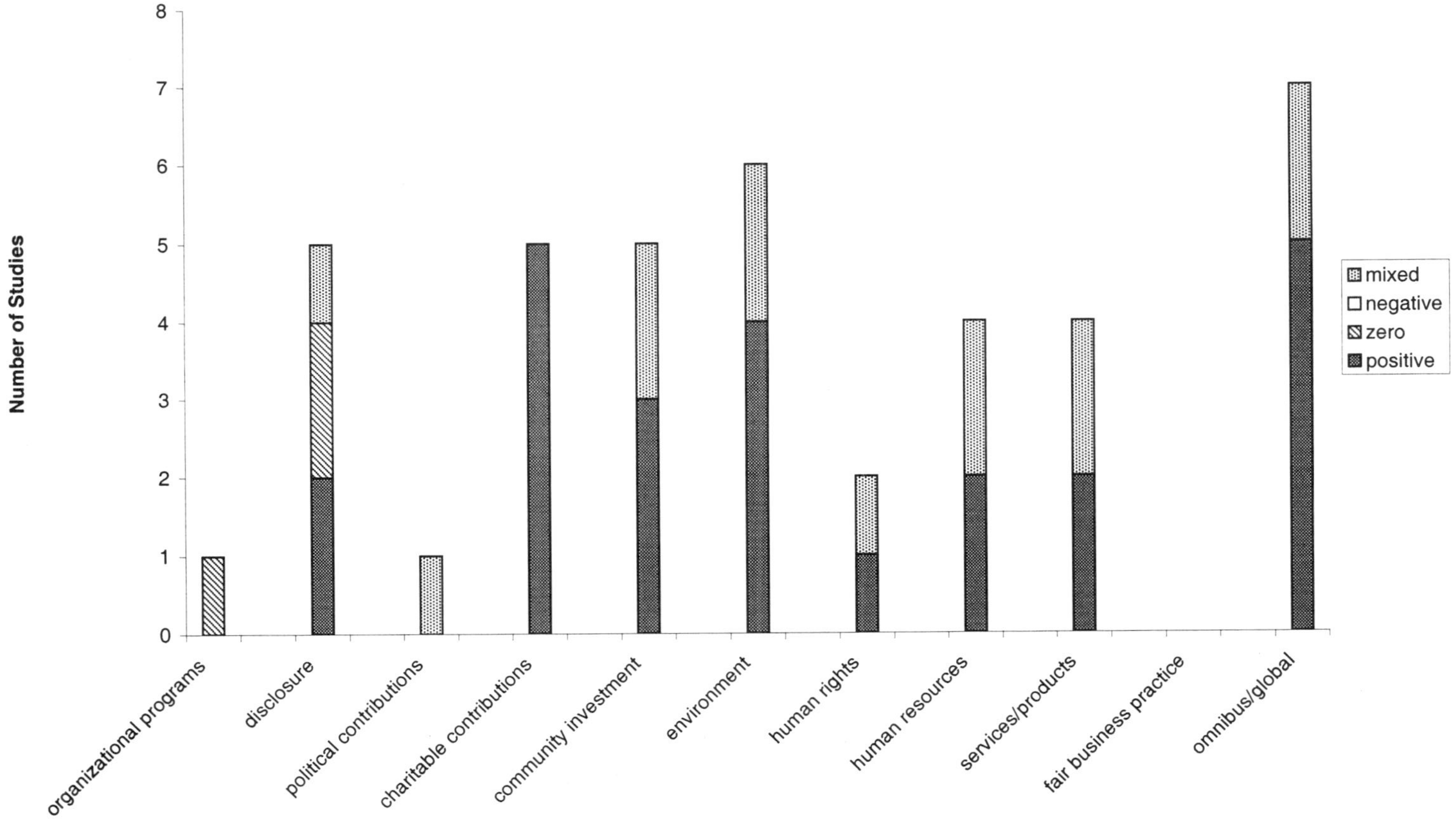

Figure 14
Results by Type of Analysis:
Corporate Social Performance as Independent Variable

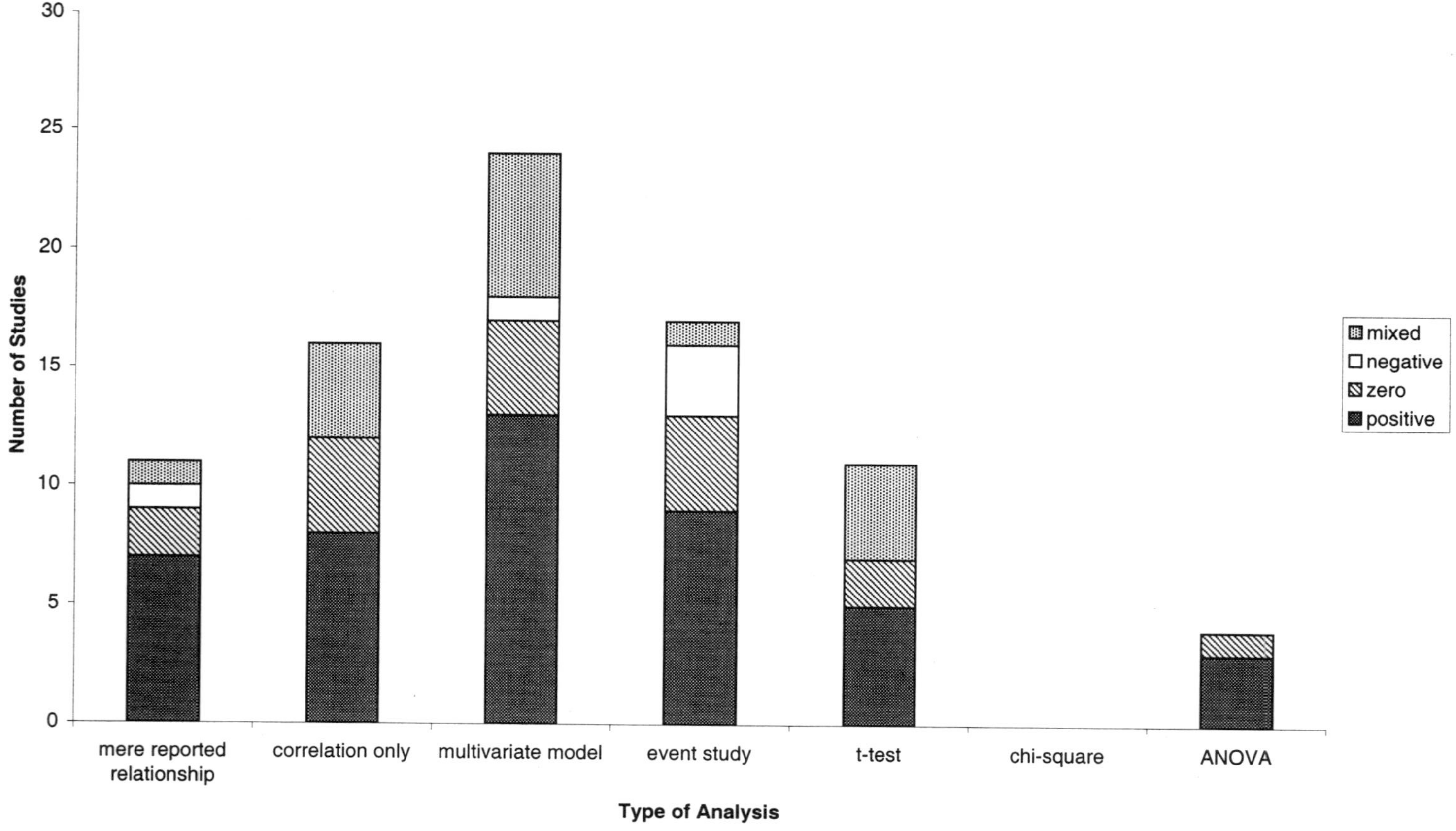

Figure 15
Results by Type of Analysis:
Corporate Social Performance as Dependent Variable

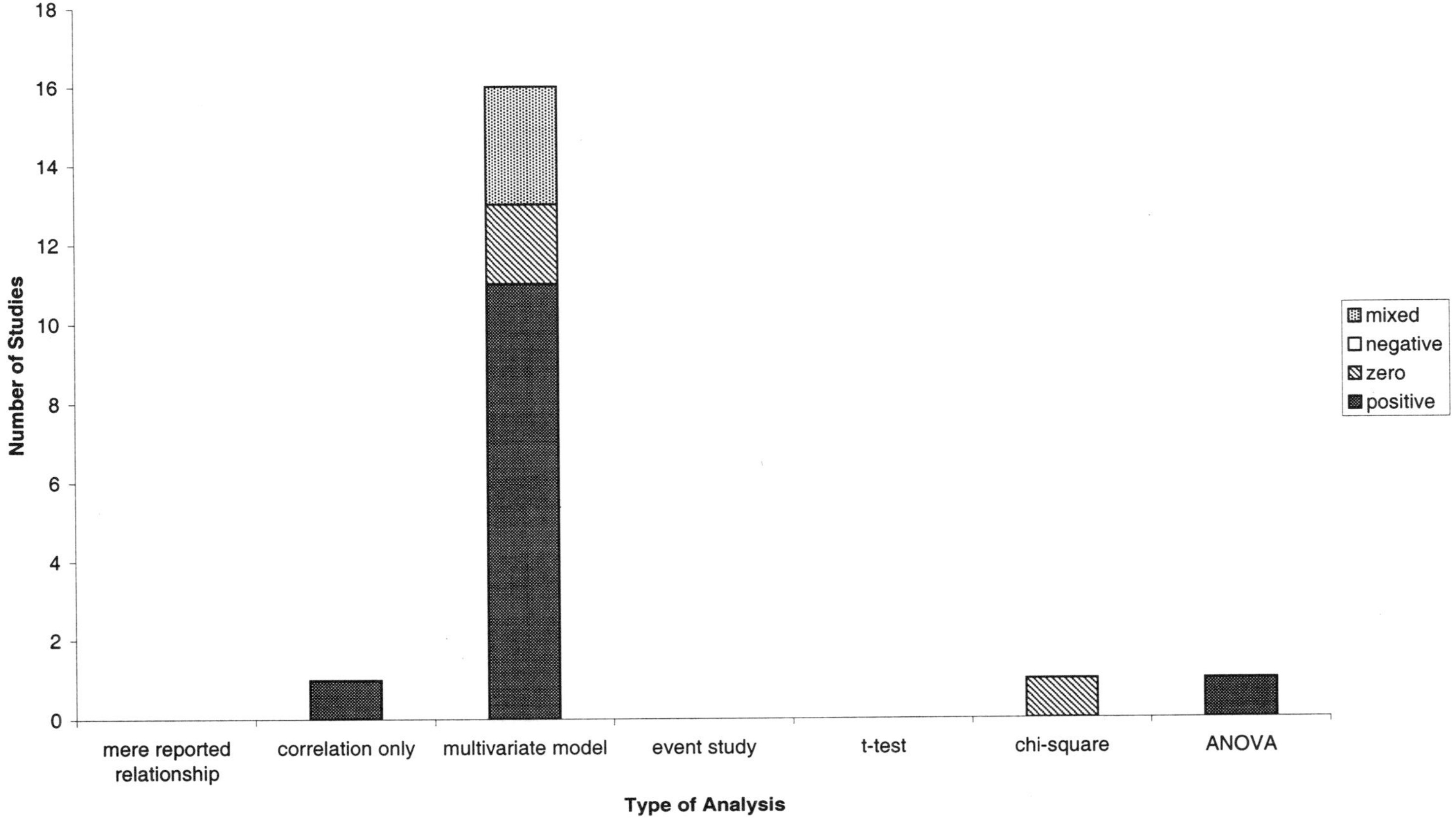

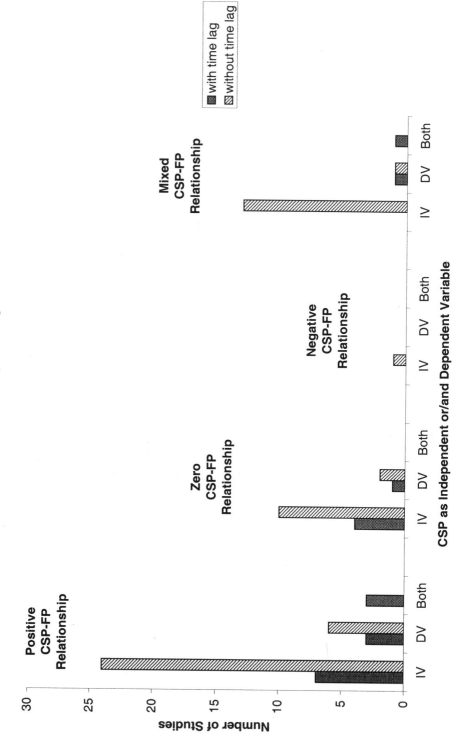

Figure 16
Results by Time Lag

Exhibit 1:
95 Studies of the Relationship between Corporate Social Performance and Financial Performance, 1972-2000

PERFORMANCE:
86 Studies

Investigator(s)	*Abbott and Monsen*
Source and year of publication	*Academy of Management Journal (1979)*
Sample size (number of companies)	450
Sample type	*Fortune 500*
Time of observation	1964-74
CSP: nature of corporate social performance investigated	social involvement disclosures
Operationalization: how CSP is measured	Ernst & Ernst's 1973 and 1974 analysis of annual reports (how many of 28 socially responsible activities were disclosed in a company's annual report)
FP: nature of financial performance	Return to Investors (a form of ROE)
Source of measured financial performance	*Fortune*
Control variable(s)	size
Analysis	content analysis
General result	0
Statistical particulars and/or summary of the data analysis	from 1964-1974, low involvement firms averaged 2.32% return, high involvement firms averaged 2.58% return (p. 523): "Being socially involved does not appear to increase investors' total rate of return. Nor does it appear that being socially involved is dysfunctional for the investor" (p. 514).
Strength of results	weak
Authors' recommendations for future research	NA

Investigator(s)	*Alexander and Buchholz*
Source and year of publication	*Academy of Management Journal (1978)*
Sample size (number of companies)	40
Sample type	Vance study
Time of observation	1970-74, 1971-73
CSP: nature of corporate social performance investigated	social reputation
Operationalization: how CSP is measured	surveys in *Business and Society Review* (same as Vance study)
FP: nature of financial performance	risk and stock return
Source of measured financial performance	risk adjusted return
Control variable(s)	risk (beta)
Analysis	rank-order correlation
General result	0
Statistical particulars and/or summary of the data analysis	correlation coefficient for 1971-73 risk-adjusted financial performance and social responsibility is .3390 (p<.05) and for 1970-74 risk and social responsibility is .2924 (p<.05); the other six correlation coefficients are n.s., and the authors conclude: "the degree of social responsibility as measured by the rankings of businessmen and students bears no significant relationship to stock market performance. Furthermore, there seems to be no significant relationship between stock risk levels and degree of social responsibility" (p. 485).
Strength of results	weak (low, non-significant relationship between performance and degree of social responsibility and between risk and degree of social responsibility)
Authors' recommendations for future research	NA

Investigator(s)	*Anderson and Frankle*
Source and year of publication	*The Accounting Review (1980)*
Sample size (number of companies)	314 (201 disclosing, 113 non-disclosing)
Sample type	*Fortune 500*
Time of observation	7/1972-6/1973
CSP: nature of corporate social performance investigated	disclosure of social performance (environmental, minority employment, personnel)
Operationalization: how CSP is measured	Ernst & Whinney's social responsibility disclosure survey
FP: nature of financial performance	beta, ROI
Source of measured financial performance	*Compustat*, Merrill Lynch Securities Research
Control variable(s)	size, dividends, earnings
Analysis	t-test (comparing monthly returns of subsets of portfolios)
General result	+
Statistical particulars and/or summary of the data analysis	socially disclosing portfolios outperform non-disclosing portfolios for the six months following fiscal year end (p<.05 for six months; p<.01 for the month of March)
Strength of results	weak (weak positive relationship for socially disclosing firms outperforming non-disclosing firms; risk of the firm does not affect performance; and market does not anticipate social disclosure prior to its release)
Authors' recommendations for future research	critical examination of what information is disclosed

Investigator(s)	*Aupperle, Carroll, and Hatfield*
Source and year of publication	*Academy of Management Journal (1985)*
Sample size (number of companies)	241 CEOs
Sample type	*Forbes 1981Annual Directory*
Time of observation	1981
CSP: nature of corporate social performance investigated	orientation toward corporate social responsibility
Operationalization: how CSP is measured	survey: (1) does the company use social forecasting? (2) is there a social responsibility committee on board of directors?
FP: nature of financial performance	ROA (short & long term; adjusted for risk)
Source of measured financial performance	risk: *Value Line* safety index
Control variable(s)	none
Analysis	(1) correlation (CEO orientation and firm performance) (2) t-tests (firms with vs. firms without social forecasts and CSR board committees)
General result	0
Statistical particulars and/or summary of the data analysis	the economic component was negatively correlated with legal (-.48), ethical (-.71), and discretionary (-.47) components yet the last three were all uncorrelated with actual financial performance
Strength of results	weak
Authors' recommendations for future research	"It could very well be that the intangible benefits of corporate social responsibility tend to evade scientific inquiry" (p. 462). Administer test to employees instead of CEOs, superior methodologies, qualitative approach

Investigator(s)	*Belkaoui*
Source and year of publication	*Financial Management (1976)*
Sample size (number of companies)	2 groups of 50 firms (100 total)
Sample type	disclosed (or did not disclose) pollution control information in annual reports
Time of observation	1969-71
CSP: nature of corporate social performance investigated	disclosure of pollution control
Operationalization: how CSP is measured	annual reports
FP: nature of financial performance	stock price
Source of measured financial performance	NA
Control variable(s)	market return: S&P 500; 50 non-disclosing companies
Analysis	rudimentary event study (regression, Mann-Whitney test)
General result	+
Statistical particulars and/or summary of the data analysis	disclosing firms perform better for 4 months after release of the annual report; the advantage is greater in the first 2 months; the market performance was better prior to the annual report release and then again after the four months
Strength of results	weak
Authors' recommendations for future research	NA

Investigator(s)	*Berman, Wicks, Kotha, and Jones*
Source and year of publication	*Academy of Management Journal (1999)*
Sample size (number of companies)	81
Sample type	81 of the top 100 firms on the 1996 *Fortune 500* (the 81 had complete data for 1991-1996; total of 486 observations)
Time of observation	1991-96
CSP: nature of corporate social performance investigated	stakeholder management (treatment of stakeholders)
Operationalization: how CSP is measured	KLD ratings for companies on: employee relations, product safety/quality, diversity, natural environment, local communities
FP: nature of financial performance	ROA
Source of measured financial performance	operating income to total assets (*Compact Disclosure*, Standard & Poor's, annual reports)
Control variable(s)	Environment Variables: Munificence (industry level sales, 1987-1995); Dynamism (standard error of the regression used to calculate munificence, divided by mean of industry sales); Power (four-firm concentration level: percentage of sales generated by the top four firms relative to total industry sales). Strategy Variables (considered part of the research question, but for CSP-FP link, can be seen as controls): efficiency (COGS/Total Sales); capital intensity (total assets/number of employees); capital expenditures (capital expenditures/sales); selling intensity (SG&A expenses/total sales)
Analysis	pooled time series (GLS)
General result	+ and 0
Statistical particulars and/or summary of the data analysis	Direct Effects: employee relations ($b=.33$, $p<.01$) and product safety/quality ($b=.27$, $p<.05$) are positively and significantly related to financial performance; diversity, natural environment, and community are not; Moderating/Interaction Effects: all five stakeholder variables had at least one statistically significant interaction with one of the strategy variables (capital intensity, selling intensity, capital expenditures, efficiency), indicating a positive association with financial performance
Strength of results	strong
Authors' recommendations for future research	survey managers to understand their motivations and intentions pertaining to strategy decisions and stakeholder orientation; a more inclusive measure of performance

48

Investigator(s)	*Blacconiere and Northcut*
Source and year of publication	*Journal of Accounting, Auditing and Finance (1997)*
Sample size (number of companies)	72
Sample type	chemical industry
Time of observation	1985-86, 1992
CSP: nature of corporate social performance investigated	(1) 1984 disclosure of environmental practices and expenditures and (2) Superfund liabilities from 1992 on
Operationalization: how CSP is measured	(1) coding information in 10K reports (2) EPA
FP: nature of financial performance	CAR (cumulative abnormal return)
Source of measured financial performance	CRSP and *Compustat*
Control variable(s)	industry, size, percentage of firm's revenue from chemical industry, sensitivity of firm-specific returns to chemical industry returns, market return
Analysis	correlation, event study
General result	+
Statistical particulars and/or summary of the data analysis	chemical firms suffer negative CARs for events related to the 1986 Superfund Amendments and Reauthorization Act (SARA), but it is less negative for chemical firms with more extensive prior disclosure of their environmental performance ($p<.1$ in 3 models, with regression coefficients around .01), and it is more negative for firms that suffered larger future EPA-reported clean-up costs ($p<.05$ in 2 models, $p<.001$ in 1 model)
Strength of results	moderate
Authors' recommendations for future research	NA

Investigator(s)	*Blacconiere and Patten*
Source and year of publication	*Journal of Accounting and Economics (1994)*
Sample size (number of companies)	47
Sample type	chemical industry
Time of observation	1983-84
CSP: nature of corporate social performance investigated	disclosure of environmental practices and expenditures
Operationalization: how CSP is measured	coding of information in 10K report
FP: nature of financial performance	CAR (cumulative abnormal returns)
Source of measured financial performance	CRSP tapes (Dec. 3-7, 1984: days surrounding the Union Carbide Bhopal explosion)
Control variable(s)	industry, size, percentage of firm's revenue from chemical industry, market return
Analysis	event study
General result	+
Statistical particulars and/or summary of the data analysis	CARs for all cases were negative, but chemical firms with more extensive prior disclosure of their environmental performance did not suffer as substantial a negative impact on stock price following the Bhopal disaster ($p<.05$ in 3 of 4 models, with parameter estimates [regression coefficients] for disclosure of .0072 and .0066) as those firms with less extensive disclosure; the intercept term ranges from -.113 to -.011. Disclosure appears only to reduce the negative impact.
Strength of results	moderate
Authors' recommendations for future research	NA

Investigator(s)	*Bowman*
Source and year of publication	*California Management Review (1978)*
Sample size (number of companies)	46
Sample type	*Dun & Bradstreet Million Dollar Directory 1975* –minicomputer and computer peripheral companies
Time of observation	1974
CSP: nature of corporate social performance investigated	corporate social responsibility
Operationalization: how CSP is measured	number of lines of discussion in the annual report, as a percentage of total lines, then coded "mention" (discussion of corporate social responsibility or identification as equal opportunity employer [EOE]) or "none" (no discussion and no mention)
FP: nature of financial performance	three-year average ROS (1972-74)
Source of measured financial performance	annual reports
Control variable(s)	industry
Analysis	binomial matched pair comparison test
General result	0
Statistical particulars and/or summary of the data analysis	8% ROS for those that mentioned vs. 5.6% for those that did not mention CSR or EOE, but the difference is non-signifant
Strength of results	Weak
Authors' recommendations for future research	NA

Investigator(s)	*Bowman and Haire*
Source and year of publication	*California Management Review (1975)*
Sample size (number of companies)	82 (51 low, 18 middle, 13 high – on Corporate Social Responsibility [CSR])
Sample type	food-processing industry
Time of observation	1969-73 (1968-72 in some cases)
CSP: nature of corporate social performance investigated	positive and negative externalities
Operationalization: how CSP is measured	proportion of lines in annual report devoted to CSR (externalities), then coded high, medium, low
FP: nature of financial performance	ROE
Source of measured financial performance	NA
Control variable(s)	size
Analysis	mere reported relationship
General result	U-shaped (medium CSR performed best financially)
Statistical particulars and/or summary of the data analysis	858 of 1,152 pairwise comparisons (74%) between medium-mention companies and those in the low and high categories showed that the medium-mention company performing better in ROE (which they take to be better than chance: "The precise confidence level figure is uncertain but the significance of the difference is not moot" [p. 53].)
Strength of results	firms with medium mention of CSR had higher profits than firms with high mention which were slightly higher than firms of low mention
Authors' recommendations for future research	comparative analysis of firm vs. industry or peer group

Investigator(s)	*Boyle, Higgins, and Rhee*
Source and year of publication	*Critical Perspectives on Accounting (1997)*
Sample size (number of companies)	64
Sample type	defense industry
Time of observation	1986
CSP: nature of corporate social performance investigated	compliance with ethical standards
Operationalization: how CSP is measured	signing the Defense Industries Initiative of July 3, 1986
FP: nature of financial performance	CAR (cumulative abnormal return)
Source of measured financial performance	CRSP
Control variable(s)	industry, other events
Analysis	event study
General result	–
Statistical particulars and/or summary of the data analysis	on the day after and the second day after the announcement, signers lost 4.83% of their value and non-signers lost 3.93% of their value (both are p<.01 when the loss is compared to zero; the difference between the two is n.s.); in the ensuing 18 months, signers lost 5.66% of their value and non-signers gained 5.42% (p<.1 for the difference between signers and non-signers)
Strength of results	moderate
Authors' recommendations for future research	NA

Investigator(s)	*Bragdon and Marlin*
Source and year of publication	*Risk Management (1972)*
Sample size (number of companies)	17
Sample type	pulp & paper industry
Time of observation	1965-71
CSP: nature of corporate social performance investigated	pollution
Operationalization: how CSP is measured	CEP
FP: nature of financial performance	(1) EPS growth, (2) ROE (average for 1965-70; 1970), Return on Capital (debt + equity) (average for 1965-70;1970)
Source of measured financial performance	*Forbes*, H.C. Wainwright & Co., Standard & Poor's
Control variable(s)	industry
Analysis	Spearman rank correlation
General result	+
Statistical particulars and/or summary of the data analysis	p<.05 for a trimmed sample of 12 firms on 10 of 15 correlation coefficients (three pollution indices and three measures of financial performance [each one run for the 5-year average and one year performance])
Strength of results	weak
Authors' recommendations for future research	study more companies

Investigator(s)	*Brown*
Source and year of publication	*Corporate Reputation Review (1997)*
Sample size (number of companies)	216 firms (940 observations)
Sample type	*Fortune* Most Admired
Time of observation	1982-92
CSP: nature of corporate social performance investigated	reputation for responsibility to the community and environment
Operationalization: how CSP is measured	Brown & Perry halo removed *Fortune* reputation database
FP: nature of financial performance	stock market returns
Source of measured financial performance	natural log of market-adjusted return (*Fortune – America's Most Admired Corporations* DataBook [1997])
Control variable(s)	past financial performance
Analysis	t-test
General result	+ and 0
Statistical particulars and/or summary of the data analysis	Companies are divided into quartiles according to their average reputation score during the period 1982-91; when the lowest reputation quartile is compared to the higest reputation quartile, for the period 1982-87, the highest quartile firms reveal a larger stock market return (p<.02; natural log of stock market return = .17) than do the lowest quartile firms (natural log of stock market return = .11); for the period 1988-92, though the lower quartile firms perform slightly better, there is no statistical difference between the highest quartile firms (natural log of stock market return = .11) and the lowest quartile (natural log of stock market return =.12); for individiual years, highest reputation quartile firms outperform lowest quartile firms in 1996 (p<.08) and 1987 (p<.05)
Strength of results	weak
Authors' recommendations for future research	NA

Investigator(s)	*Brown*
Source and year of publication	*Corporate Reputation Review (1998)*
Sample size (number of companies)	149-197 firms (323-2370 observations)
Sample type	*Fortune Most Admired*
Time of observation	1982-91
CSP: nature of corporate social performance investigated	reputation for responsibility to the community and environment
Operationalization: how CSP is measured	Brown & Perry halo-removed *Fortune* reputation database
FP: nature of financial performance	stock market returns
Source of measured financial performance	natural log of market-adjusted return *(Fortune – America's Most Admired Corporations DataBook [1997])*
Control variable(s)	
Analysis	correlation and regression
General result	+
Statistical particulars and/or summary of the data analysis	CSP reputation coefficient = .022 (p<.05) when cumulative annual market return (1984-96) is regressed on it; that is, for every point in reputation, a firm gains an additional 2.2% return
Strength of results	moderate
Authors' recommendations for future research	NA

Investigator(s)	*Chen and Metcalf*
Source and year of publication	*The Accounting Review (1980)*
Sample size (number of companies)	18
Sample type	pulp & paper industry
Time of observation	1968-73, 1969-71, 1971-73
CSP: nature of corporate social performance investigated	pollution control
Operationalization: how CSP is measured	pollution control indices based on information from CEP
FP: nature of financial performance	profit, size, total and systematic risk, price/earnings ratio
Source of measured financial performance	*Compustat*
Control variable(s)	size of firm
Analysis	product-moment correlation, partial correlation, regression
General result	0
Statistical particulars and/or summary of the data analysis	demonstrate that Spicer found a spurious relationship
Strength of results	they spend their entire study trying to prove Spicer wrong (which they think they did) but there is no real way to determine the validity of their results since they employed little to no statistical analyses
Authors' recommendations for future research	further disclosure of CSP is unnecessary; CSP is a concern for investors insofar as it benefits earnings

Investigator(s)	*Christmann*
Source and year of publication	*Academy of Management Journal* (2000)
Sample size (number of companies)	88
Sample type	business units of chemical companies
Time of observation	1996
CSP: nature of corporate social performance investigated	environmental practices .
Operationalization: how CSP is measured	survey responses
FP: nature of financial performance	cost advantage
Source of measured financial performance	survey responses
Control variable(s)	industry, type of environmental issue addressed by operations innovation
Analysis	OLS
General result	+
Statistical particulars and/or summary of the data analysis	proprietary pollution prevention innovations reduce costs (b=.19, p<.1), and the effect is augmented when a firm has high levels of complementary assets (b=.24, p<.1 for the interaction effect); early timing of environmental strategies gain larger cost advantages for firms with high levels of complementary assets (b=.22, p<.05 for the interaction effect)
Strength of results	modest
Authors' recommendations for future research	investigate firms' environmental strategies within the context of broader resources, capabilities, and strategies that a firm possesses; investigate the practices, resources, and capabilities of firms that fail to gain competitive advantage from environmental strategies

Investigator(s)	*Clarkson*
Source and year of publication	Research in Corporate Social Performance and Policy (1980)
Sample size (number of companies)	32
Sample type	Canadian companies
Time of observation	1983-86
CSP: nature of corporate social performance investigated	at least 29 items covering human resources, environment, charity, community relations, customer relations, and organizational practices and structures
Operationalization: how CSP is measured	case studies that provided basis on which companies are rated along the multiple dimensions
FP: nature of financial performance	rating of 1 to 4 relative to industry
Source of measured financial performance	unspecified
Control variable(s)	none
Analysis	mere reported association
General result	+
Statistical particulars and/or summary of the data analysis	17 of 32 companies "show social orientation as proactive and have above average economic performance" (p. 257)
Strength of results	weak
Authors' recommendations for future research	apply this method to evaluate non-profit and governmental organizations and to extend and validate findings of this study

Investigator(s)	*Cochran and Wood*
Source and year of publication	*Academy of Management Journal (1984)*
Sample size (number of companies)	(1)39 (2)36
Sample type	Moskowitz's list
Time of observation	1970-74, 1975-79
CSP: nature of corporate social performance investigated	social reputation
Operationalization: how CSP is measured	Moskowitz's three tiers (best, honorable mention, worst)
FP: nature of financial performance	accounting measures (ROA – operating earnings/assets, ROS – earnings/sales), EV (excess market valuation), asset turnover, asset age
Source of measured financial performance	*Compustat*
Control variable(s)	industry
Analysis	regression, logit analysis
General result	+ and 0
Statistical particulars and/or summary of the data analysis	mixed results for ROS and ROA; when asset age is included in the model, only 1975-79 ROS is significantly different ($p<.05$) between "honorable mention" and "worst" categories; strongest relationship is between asset age and CSR: older assets are associated with lower CSR ratings; omitting asset age suggests that a spurious correlation may exist between CSR and the financial performance indicators
Strength of results	weak (key correlate with CSR is asset age not profit [only weak support for association between CSR and measures of financial performance]); "there is still weak support for a link between CSR and financial performance" (p. 55)
Authors' recommendations for future research	"better measures of CSR are desperately needed. It may never be possible to measure CSR objectively. Therefore research in this area could focus on *perceptions* of CSR" (p. 55, italics in original); direction of causation; additional explanatory variables

PERFORMANCE

Investigator(s)	*Conine and Madden*
Source and year of publication	*Handbook of Business Strategy: 1986/1987 Yearbook (1986-87)*
Sample size (number of companies)	163
Sample type	*Fortune Most Admired*
Time of observation	1983-85
CSP: nature of corporate social performance investigated	reputation for responsibility to the community and environment
Operationalization: how CSP is measured	*Fortune* corporate reputation study (1 of 8 attributes): current and change in expectation
FP: nature of financial performance	performance reputation
Source of measured financial performance	*Fortune* corporate reputation study (7 attributes, including long-term investment value): current and change in expectation
Control variable(s)	risk
Analysis	correlation
General result	+
Statistical particulars and/or summary of the data analysis	p<.01
Strength of results	moderate
Authors' recommendations for future research	study industry specific characteristics, better measure of CSR

61

Investigator(s)	*Cottrill*
Source and year of publication	*Journal of Business Ethics (1990)*
Sample size (number of companies)	180
Sample type	18 industries
Time of observation	1982-83
CSP: nature of corporate social performance investigated	social reputation
Operationalization: how CSP is measured	*Fortune* corporate reputation study
FP: nature of financial performance	industry, industry competition, market power
Source of measured financial performance	*Compustat* (2-digit SIC, concentration ratio, market share)
Control variable(s)	industry
Analysis	ANOVA, regression
General result	+
Statistical particulars and/or summary of the data analysis	F-tests (p<.0001), industry influences CSR
Strength of results	moderate
Authors' recommendations for future research	expand the sample while generating more defensible market share and concentration numbers

Investigator(s)	*Diltz*
Source and year of publication	*Applied Financial Economics (1995)*
Sample size (number of companies)	159 large US firms in a variety of industries
Sample type	All firms cross-listed by CEP and CRSP in this time period
Time of observation	CEP's 1991 published assessments (unclear CSP evaluation date) and 1989 – 91 for CRSP financial data
CSP: nature of corporate social performance investigated	CSR ("ethical screening")
Operationalization: how CSP is measured	CEP Index (environment, charitable giving, women in management, minority management, animal testing, information disclosure, community outreach, South Africa, family benefits, military work, nuclear involvement)
FP: nature of financial performance	Jensen's alpha (with value-weighted market indices) and abnormal returns (with a wide variety of estimation windows)
Source of measured financial performance	CRSP
Control variable(s)	risk
Analysis	event study (with varying event dates), t-tests
General result	+/0/-
Statistical particulars and/or summary of the data analysis	"Our findings provide evidence to suggest that ethical screening of firms has little impact on portfolio returns. To the extent that ethical screening has any effect, the market appears to reward good environmental performances, charitable giving, and an absence of nuclear work, and it appears to penalize firms that provide family-related benefits such as parental leave, job sharing, and dependent care assistance" (pp. 69-70). He reports 182 different t-tests in the paper; 22 are statistically significant (9 would be expected by chance at the .05 level).
Strength of results	Weak
Authors' recommendations for future research	NA

Investigator(s)	*Dowell, Hart, and Yeung*
Source and year of publication	*Management Science 2000*
Sample size (number of companies)	89
Sample type	manufacturing and mining firms in S&P 500
Time of observation	1994-97
CSP: nature of corporate social performance investigated	environmental practices
Operationalization: how CSP is measured	Investor Responsibility Research Center's Corporate Environmental Profile: companies' adherence to environmental standards (local, U.S., stringent global)
FP: nature of financial performance	Tobin's q (firm market value per dollar of replacement costs of tangible assets; that is, outstanding shares times share price, plus book value of long term debt, plus net current liabilities, divided by the sum of book value of inventory plus net value of physical plant and equipment)
Source of measured financial performance	*Compustat*
Control variable(s)	R&D intensity, advertising intensity, leverage, size, multinationality (percent of foreign assets)
Analysis	regression
General result	+
Statistical particulars and/or summary of the data analysis	companies adhering to stringent global environmental standards outperform companies adhering to U.S. or local standards (p<.05 or above in four models); Tobin's q differences reveal that those adhering to stringent global standards enjoy $8.6 billion more per firm in value than those adhering to U.S. standards abroad
Strength of results	strong
Authors' recommendations for future research	longer time-frame for doing analysis; more fine-grained measure of companies' presence in developing countries; identify the motivation behind the changes in environmental standards

Investigator(s)	*Fogler and Nutt*
Source and year of publication	*Academy of Management Journal (1975)*
Sample size (number of companies)	9
Sample type	Subset of firms in Bradgon and Marlin study
Time of observation	3/1971-3/1972
CSP: nature of corporate social performance investigated	pollution control
Operationalization: how CSP is measured	pollution indices from CEP
FP: nature of financial performance	(1)price/earnings, (2)mutual fund purchases, (3)short run price performance
Source of measured financial performance	(1)quarterly reports, (2)*Value Line* (3) stock prices
Control variable(s)	industry (pulp & paper)
Analysis	regression
General result	(1)0 (2) 0 (3) 0
Statistical particulars and/or summary of the data analysis	(1) negative coefficient but non-significant, (3) rudimentary event study
Strength of results	Weak
Authors' recommendations for future research	"it may be premature to advise managers on the functional relationship between social responsibility and present value maximization" (p.159)

Investigator(s)	*Freedman and Jaggi*
Source and year of publication	*Omega (1982)*
Sample size (number of companies)	109
Sample type	polluting industries (steel, oil, pulp & paper)
Time of observation	1973-74
CSP: nature of corporate social performance investigated	pollution control
Operationalization: how CSP is measured	CEP Index
FP: nature of financial performance	ROA, ROE, cash basis ROA and ROE, operating ratio
Source of measured financial performance	NA
Control variable(s)	type of company
Analysis	Spearman rank correlation, Pearson product-moment correlation
General result	0
Statistical particulars and/or summary of the data analysis	largest quartile of firms: higher ROE correlated with poor disclosures
Strength of results	weak
Authors' recommendations for future research	NA

PERFORMANCE

Investigator(s)	*Freedman and Jaggi*
Source and year of publication	*Advances in Public Interest Accounting (1986)*
Sample size (number of companies)	88 total, 56 in statistical tests
Sample type	highly polluting industries (chemical, pulp & paper, oil refining, steel)
Time of observation	1973-74
CSP: nature of corporate social performance investigated	degree of pollution disclosure in 10Ks and Annual Reports
Operationalization: how CSP is measured	weighting scheme for six different pieces of information (firm's performance on EPA emissions standards; future capital expenditures; current capital expenditures; past capital expenditures; descriptive data with percentages; descriptive data alone)
FP: nature of financial performance	stock price performance
Source of measured financial performance	Sharpe-Lintner market model of returns following filing month of 10K
Control variable(s)	stock market performance, industry
Analysis	event study
General result	0
Statistical particulars and/or summary of the data analysis	firms with extensive disclosure of their pollution performance did not differ significantly in stock price performance from firms with minimal disclosure
Strength of results	moderate
Authors' recommendations for future research	create a standard format in corporate reports for disclosing environmental information

67

Investigator(s)	*Freedman and Stagliano*
Source and year of publication	*Accounting, Auditing & Accountability Journal (1991)*
Sample size (number of companies)	27
Sample type	textile companies (subject to Supreme Court decision permitting stricter OSHA dust emission regulations)
Time of observation	6/17-6/20/1981
CSP: nature of corporate social performance investigated	material costs of adhering to OSHA and EPA regulations
Operationalization: how CSP is measured	10K disclosures of potential costs associated with the stricter rule, coded into four categories (no disclosure, report no material effect, narrative assessment, and quantitative assessment)
FP: nature of financial performance	mean abnormal return
Source of measured financial performance	CRSP
Control variable(s)	risk, industry
Analysis	event study
General result	+
Statistical particulars and/or summary of the data analysis	"market valuations of firms which provided no disclosure, only narrative commentary, or which described the standard as not materially affecting their operations, declined relative to firms that disclosed quantitative information about the potential implications of the standard" (p. 80); $p<.1$ for OLS method, revealing a 1.2% decline on the announcement day for all firms not in the quantitative disclosing category, relative to the quantitative disclosers; $p<.05$ for WLS method; $p<.1$ (1.3% decline) and $p<.01$ (1.7% decline) for days 0 and +2, respectively, for the WLS method, and $p<.01$ (2.3% decline) for the OLS method on day +2
Strength of results	moderate to strong
Authors' recommendations for future research	NA

Investigator(s)	*Fry and Hock*
Source and year of publication	Business and Society Review (1976)
Sample size (number of companies)	135 firms
Sample type	self-selected sample (15 industries, company sales from $2 million to $1 billion)
Time of observation	NA
CSP: nature of corporate social performance investigated	social responsiveness
Operationalization: how CSP is measured	(1) photographs in annual report, (2) references in annual report to expenditures on pollution abatement, affirmative action, energy conservation, community involvement, charity, product safety (they gave points to paragraphs/photos that spoke to these themes)
FP: nature of financial performance	assets, earnings, sales, equity, ROI
Source of measured financial performance	annual reports
Control variable(s)	public image of the industry (as rated by business students)
Analysis	NA
General result	0
Statistical particulars and/or summary of the data analysis	no statistical analysis; they report: "The most important factor in determining the annual report space allocated to social responsibility activities is the size of the company. The second most important variable is the type of industry the company is in. Earnings are a poor third" (pp. 63-64). ". . .companies in industries with the worst public image were giving the greatest emphasis to responsiveness" (p. 64).
Strength of results	weak
Authors' recommendations for future research	NA

Investigator(s)	*Fry, Keim, and Meiners*
Source and year of publication	*Academy of Management Journal (1982)*
Sample size (number of companies)	36 industry groupings and subset of 6 rated highest or lowest in public contact
Sample type	high contact: insurance, hotel, merchandise stores; low contact: mining, construction, metals
Time of observation	1946-73
CSP: nature of corporate social performance investigated	philanthropy
Operationalization: how CSP is measured	IRS
FP: nature of financial performance	business expenses: advertising, employee benefits, pension contributions, distribution to stockholders, compensation to officers
Source of measured financial performance	IRS data
Control variable(s)	industry groupings, public contact
Analysis	regression, analysis of covariance through multiple regression (ANCOVA)
General result	+: key finding for CSP-FP relationship: dividend increases predict increases in philanthropic giving. For 36 industries: (1) expenditures on advertising and philanthropy move together; (2) changes in contributions correlate with changes in other business expenses. For high public contact vs. low contact: (1) for both: contributions increase relative to advertising as income increases; (2) high public contact companies spend more than low on contributions
Statistical particulars and/or summary of the data analysis	p<.01 for all results
Strength of results	strong
Authors' recommendations for future research	"positive analysis of social issues should precede normative discussions in this emotive area" (p. 105)

PERFORMANCE

Investigator(s)	*Galaskiewicz*
Source and year of publication	*Administrative Science Quarterly (1997)*
Sample size (number of companies)	(1) 69, (2) 73, (3) 39
Sample type	Minneapolis-St. Paul
Time of observation	(1)1979-81 (2)1979-89 (3) both periods
CSP: nature of corporate social performance investigated	charitable donations
Operationalization: how CSP is measured	foundation disbursements and direct cash contributions
FP: nature of financial performance	three steps: (1) calculated six ratios: pretax net income as a percentage of sales, assets, and equity and after tax net income as a percentage of sales, assets, and equity; (2) then coded each company based on which quartile its after-tax measures fell into versus its industry; (3) then averaged each company's rank on the various measures (p. 455)
Source of measured financial performance	*Corporate Report Factbook, Dun and Bradstreet's Million Dollar Directory, Standard & Poor's Register of Corporations*
Control variable(s)	industry, size
Analysis	regression (OLS)
General result	+
Statistical particulars and/or summary of the data analysis	p<.05 for effect of financial performance on philanthropic contributions (for both time periods independently and together); p<.01 for the effect of changes in financial performance on philanthropic contributions
Strength of results	strong: adjusted R-squareds of .707 and .833 for the two time periods
Authors' recommendations for future research	informal social structures are as important as formal civic organizations and firm performance in getting companies to make charitable contributions

Investigator(s)	*Graves and Waddock*
Source and year of publication	*Business and Society Review* (forthcoming)
Sample size (number of companies)	22
Sample type	11 of the original 18 pairs of companies in Collins and Porras's *Built to Last*
Time of observation	1989-97
CSP: nature of corporate social performance investigated	"the way that companies treat their primary stakeholders" (p. 12): community relations, employee relations, environment, product, diversity
Operationalization: how CSP is measured	KLD
FP: nature of financial performance	accounting: ROE, ROA, ROS, debt/assets; market: 10-year total return relative to industry, 10-year total return
Source of measured financial performance	*Compustat*
Control variable(s)	industry, paired sample
Analysis	t-test
General result	+
Statistical particulars and/or summary of the data analysis	pooled t-tests for the years 1991-97 reveal statistically significant differences between *Built to Last* companies and their pairs on community relations ($p<.01$), employee relations ($p<.052$), environment ($p<.052$), product ($p<.0001$), diversity ($p<.0001$) and CSP average ($p<.0001$); pooled t-tests for the years 1989-96 reveal statistically significant differences between *Built to Last* companies and their pairs on ROE ($p<.0003$), ROA ($p<.0001$), ROS ($p<.0004$), 10-year return relative to industry ($p<.0001$), 10-year total return ($p<.0001$), and debt/assets ($p<.05$); differences in Beta were non-significant.
Strength of results	moderate
Authors' recommendations for future research	

Investigator(s)	*Graves and Waddock*
Source and year of publication	*Academy of Management Journal (1994)*
Sample size (number of companies)	430
Sample type	S&P 500
Time of observation	1990
CSP: nature of corporate social performance investigated	corporate social performance
Operationalization: how CSP is measured	index developed from data in KLD
FP: nature of financial performance	institutional ownership
Source of measured financial performance	S&P Stock Guides (mid-1991)
Control variable(s)	firm profitability (ROA, ROE), size (total assets, total sales), debt level (long-term debt/total assets), industry (4-digit SIC)
Analysis	regression
General result	+ and 0
Statistical particulars and/or summary of the data analysis	Table 1 reports correlations: .15 for CSP and ROA (p<.01), .03 for CSP and ROE (n.s.); for number of institutions holding shares, coefficient for CSP ranges from .11 (p<.01) to .15 (p<.001); for percent of shares owned by institutional investors, no results are significant
Strength of results	strong, support for the association between CSP and institutional ownership (also found that lower risk-adjusted discount rate increases investment and can be brought about by greater CSP)
Authors' recommendations for future research	NA

Investigator(s)	*Griffin and Mahon*
Source and year of publication	*Business & Society (1997)*
Sample size (number of companies)	7
Sample type	chemical industry
Time of observation	1992
CSP: nature of corporate social performance investigated	4 measures: 2 perceptual and 2 concrete data
Operationalization: how CSP is measured	perceptions: 1992 *Fortune* corporate reputation survey and KLD indices; concrete data: 1992 Toxics Release Inventory (EPA) & charitable contributions (*Corporate 500 Directory of Corporate Philanthropy*)
FP: nature of financial performance	ROA, ROE, TA (total assets) asset age, 5 year ROS (1987-1992)
Source of measured financial performance	*1994 Compact Disclosure,* 1992 annual reports
Control variable(s)	industry
Analysis	each company is assigned a relative rank for each measure of CSP and financial performance, then an average rank is calculated, and then CSP and financial performance are compared
General result	+
Statistical particulars and/or summary of the data analysis	no statistical analyses were conducted - Table 4 shows a 3X3 matrix (CSP by financial performance: high, medium, low) and while there is a company that fits into most every cell, "there are no firms in the high corporate social performance and low corporate financial performance block" (p.26)
Strength of results	weak
Authors' recommendations for future research	consistency: focus on one industry at a time, focus on multiple – but only a few key CSP and CFP measurements, look at the relationship over time

PERFORMANCE

Investigator(s)	*Guerard*
Source and year of publication	*Journal of Investing (1997a)*
Sample size (number of companies)	2,250 stocks (950 socially screened, 1,300 unscreened)
Sample type	Vantage Global Advisors
Time of observation	1987-94
CSP: nature of corporate social performance investigated	screened stock portfolio
Operationalization: how CSP is measured	Vantage Global Advisors less KLD exclusions
FP: nature of financial performance	total returns
Source of measured financial performance	quarterly returns
Control variable(s)	NA
Analysis	quarterly regressions
General result	0
Statistical particulars and/or summary of the data analysis	quarterly returns: unscreened 1.068% vs. 1.057% CSR-screened; authors interpret this as positive for CSR since there is no statistical difference ("There continues to be no meaningful cost to implementing social screens" [p.16])
Strength of results	NA
Authors' recommendations for future research	NA

Investigator(s)	*Guerard*
Source and year of publication	Journal of Investing (1997b)
Sample size (number of companies)	950
Sample type	1,200 stocks in Vantage Global Advisors universe, less KLD exclusions
Time of observation	1987-95
CSP: nature of corporate social performance investigated	KLD screens
Operationalization: how CSP is measured	KLD criteria: product, environment, military, nuclear power, employee relations, women and minorities, South Africa
FP: nature of financial performance	excess market return
Source of measured financial performance	average monthly returns (Vantage Global Advisors, S&P 500)
Control variable(s)	market return
Analysis	comparison of return, regression
General result	+ and 0 and −
Statistical particulars and/or summary of the data analysis	screened portfolio outperforms unscreened portfolio (743 basis points of excess return vs. 638, with the 1200 vs. 950 stock sample; 572 basis points of excess return vs. 450 for the S&P 500 sample); KLD product criterion has a positive and significant relationship with performance in 1992, 1994, 1996 (sig. Level is not reported), and the military criterion has a negative and significant relationship with performance in 1993-1994; all other KLD criteria have no significant association with subsequent returns
Strength of results	moderate
Authors' recommendations for future research	NA

Investigator(s)	*Hamilton, Jo and Statman*
Source and year of publication	*Financial Analysts Journal (1993)*
Sample size (number of companies)	17 (funds established in or before 1985), 15 (funds established after 1985)
Sample type	socially responsible mutual funds
Time of observation	1/1981- 12/1990
CSP: nature of corporate social performance investigated	social reputation
Operationalization: how CSP is measured	equity mutual funds identified by their managers as socially responsible
FP: nature of financial performance	stock market performance (excess return on funds)
Source of measured financial performance	Lipper Analytical Services
Control variable(s)	fund age
Analysis	t-test on Jensen's alpha
General result	0
Statistical particulars and/or summary of the data analysis	no statistical difference in performance of responsible and conventional funds ("social responsibility factors have no effect on expected stock returns or companies' cost of capital" [p. 66])
Strength of results	modest
Authors' recommendations for future research	NA

Investigator(s)	*Hart and Ahuja*
Source and year of publication	*Business Strategy and the Environment (1996)*
Sample size (number of companies)	127
Sample type	S&P 500 (involved in manufacturing, mining, or production)
Time of observation	1988-92 (emissions reduction from 1988 to 1989; financial performance for 1989-92)
CSP: nature of corporate social performance investigated	environmental performance
Operationalization: how CSP is measured	emissions reduction (reported by Investor Responsibility Research Center)
FP: nature of financial performance	ROS, ROA, ROE
Source of measured financial performance	*Compustat*
Control variable(s)	R&D intensity, advertising intensity, capital intensity, leverage, industry, size (removed from regression)
Analysis	lagged regression (OLS)
General result	+
Statistical particulars and/or summary of the data analysis	emissions reduction in period t enhances operating performance (ROS, ROA) in periods t+1 ($p<.05$) and t+2 ($p<.01$ for ROS; $p<.05$ for ROA) and t+3 ($p<.05$); emissions reduction in period t enhances financial performance (ROE) in period t+2 ($p<.05$) and t+3 ($p<.05$); emissions reduction in time period t shows no relationship to operating or financial performance in that same time period
Strength of results	moderate
Authors' recommendations for future research	investigate direction of causality; look beyond just lowering production of emissions to measure whether it pays to be green; target specific industry sectors; finer grained approaches to measuring emissions reduction

Investigator(s)	*Heinze*
Source and year of publication	*Akron Business and Economic Review (1976)*
Sample size (number of companies)	28
Sample type	National Affiliation of Concerned Business Students (NACBS) rating of U.S. corporations
Time of observation	1972
CSP: nature of corporate social performance investigated	social involvement
Operationalization: how CSP is measured	NACBS ratings (1 to 5 scale)
FP: nature of financial performance	growth, income/sales, operating profit/sales, current ratio, capitalization, income/assets, income/worth
Source of measured financial performance	*NA*
Control variable(s)	none
Analysis	regression and case study
General result	+
Statistical particulars and/or summary of the data analysis	R-squared of .43 (for model in which Social Involvement Rating is predicted by 7 financial variables)
Strength of results	moderate
Authors' recommendations for future research	NA

Investigator(s)	*Herremans, Akathaporn, McInnes*
Source and year of publication	*Accounting, Organizations and Society (1993)*
Sample size (number of companies)	76 for stock market returns and 96 for accounting measures
Sample type	*Fortune Most Admired*
Time of observation	1982-87
CSP: nature of corporate social performance investigated	responsibility to the community and environment (high and low groups)
Operationalization: how CSP is measured	the one *Fortune* corporate reputation survey criterion on responsiveness to community and environmental issues (authors then categorized companies as "good" [score of 1-5 in every year 1982-87] or "poor" [score >5 for every year 1982-87])
FP: nature of financial performance	4 accounting indicators: operating margin, net margin, ROA, ROE; abnormal stock market return; risk
Source of measured financial performance	*Compustat*, CRSP
Control variable(s)	extent of social conflict in the industry, size, leverage
Analysis	"analysis of differences" and correlations
General result	+
Statistical particulars and/or summary of the data analysis	operating margin, net margin, ROA, ROE: significant difference between companies rated as more responsible than those rated less responsible (p<.05 and p<.1, depending on the year) for companies in industries characterized by more social conflict; risk: significant difference between more and less responsible companies in both categories of industries; stock market performance (abnormal returns): significant difference for companies in industries with more social conflict and in 1987, companies rated more responsible in the low-conflict industries performed worse
Strength of results	moderate
Authors' recommendations for future research	NA

Investigator(s)	*Holman, New, and Singer*
Source and year of publication	*Corporation and Society Research: Studies in Theory and Measurement (1990)*
Sample size (number of companies)	49 (steel, pulp & paper, textiles, rubber)
Sample type	*Fortune 500*
Time of observation	1973-77
CSP: nature of corporate social performance investigated	(1) content analysis and (2) expenditures
Operationalization: how CSP is measured	(1)number of mentions in annual reports of activity in environment, energy, fair business practices, human resources, community involvement, products, and other; (2) index of estimated expenditures for regulatory compliance reported in federal regulatory analysis reports, as a portion of total capital expenditures
FP: nature of financial performance	(1) total risk (2) systematic risk
Source of measured financial performance	NA
Control variable(s)	leverage, industry, payout ratio, acid-test ratio
Analysis	regression
General result	(1) + for total risk regressed on expenditures, (2) 0 for the three other relationships (total and systematic risk regressed on mentions; systematic risk regressed on expenditures)
Statistical particulars and/or summary of the data analysis	$p<.01$ for expenditures and total risk, with a rise of .21 in adjusted R-squared: "Disclosure of high environmental cost requirements has an adverse impact on shareholder wealth or firm value" (p. 277)
Strength of results	moderate (one result is strong, but none of the others is significant)
Authors' recommendations for future research	expand mandatory corporate disclosure in areas of social performance, focusing on potential costs; "managers need to anticipate where the government will regulate and develop strategies for reporting and compliance focused on the long-run" (p. 278)

Investigator(s)	*Ingram*
Source and year of publication	*Journal of Accounting Research (1978)*
Sample size (number of companies)	287
Sample type	*Fortune 500*
Time of observation	5/1/1970-4/30/1976
CSP: nature of corporate social performance investigated	monetary and non-monetary social responsibility disclosures
Operationalization: how CSP is measured	annual reports
FP: nature of financial performance	cumulative excess returns (CER)
Source of measured financial performance	*Compustat*
Control variable(s)	firm excess earnings, industry, fiscal year
Analysis	regression and t-tests
General result	+
Statistical particulars and/or summary of the data analysis	"In most cases, the firms which made social responsibility disclosures outperformed those which did not" (p. 280); statistical evidence reveals that the results are significant but only when you look at industry segments
Strength of results	moderate
Authors' recommendations for future research	evaluate information content by analyzing the impact of the signals on the market instead of a general cross-section of firms

Investigator(s)	*Ingram and Frazier*
Source and year of publication	*Journal of Business Research (1983)*
Sample size (number of companies)	79
Sample type	metal manufacturing and fabricating, oil, chemicals
Time of observation	1978
CSP: nature of corporate social performance investigated	disclosure of environmental quality control
Operationalization: how CSP is measured	content analysis of president's letter in annual report (along 8 dimensions, only one of which – environmental quality – is relevant here)
FP: nature of financial performance	48 ratios falling into three factors: ROI, capital intensiveness, and financial leverage
Source of measured financial performance	*Compustat*
Control variable(s)	firm size, percentage of voting stock held by institutions
Analysis	stepwise regression
General result	0
Statistical particulars and/or summary of the data analysis	non-significant relationship between disclosure of environmental quality control and all financial variables (as well as controls)
Strength of results	weak to modest
Authors' recommendations for future research	NA

Investigator(s)	*Johnson and Greening*
Source and year of publication	*Academy of Management Journal (1999)*
Sample size (number of companies)	252
Sample type	from 1993 KLD database
Time of observation	1991-93
CSP: nature of corporate social performance investigated	KLD dimensions divided into two factors: (1) people dimension: community, women and minorities, employee relations; (2) product quality: environment, product quality
Operationalization: how CSP is measured	KLD ratings coded from –2 to +2
FP: nature of financial performance	accounting (1991-92 averages): ROA, ROE, ROS
Source of measured financial performance	*Compustat*, proxy statements
Control variable(s)	size, industry
Analysis	structural equation model with confirmatory factor analysis
General result	0 and +
Statistical particulars and/or summary of the data analysis	accounting measures positively associated with "people dimensions" (community, minorities, employee relations) (loading of .23, p<.01) but zero association with "product quality dimension" (environment, product quality) (loading of .06, n.s.); pension funds and outside directors: + for "people" and "product quality"; top management equity: + for "product quality"
Strength of results	moderate: .23 (p<.01) for impact of firm performance on "people"
Authors' recommendations for future research	examine indirect relationships between institutional investors and CSP; have a more fine-grained analysis of pension funds

Investigator(s)	*Judge and Douglas*
Source and year of publication	*Journal of Management Studies (1998)*
Sample size (number of companies)	196 responses (170 in table)
Sample type	questionnaire sample with median of 6,000 employees and range of 20 to 430,000 employees
Time of observation	1993 (1992 *World Environmental Directory* is cited)
CSP: nature of corporate social performance investigated	environment
Operationalization: how CSP is measured	self-report (1-5 scale vs. industry for: legal compliance, limit impact beyond compliance, prevent and mitigate crises, educate employees and public)
FP: nature of financial performance	ROI, earnings growth, sales growth, market share change
Source of measured financial performance	self-report survey (1 to 5 scale vs. industry)
Control variable(s)	size (employees)
Analysis	structural equation model (LISREL)
General result	+
Statistical particulars and/or summary of the data analysis	degree of environmental issues integration is associated: + (.558, p<.01) with environmental performance; + (.265, p<.01) with financial performance
Strength of results	strong
Authors' recommendations for future research	longitudinal and case studies

Investigator(s)	*Kedia and Kuntz*
Source and year of publication	Research in Corporate Social Performance and Policy (1981)
Sample size (number of companies)	30
Sample type	Texas commercial banks (stratified random sample from *Texas Red Book*)
Time of observation	1977
CSP: nature of corporate social performance investigated	socially responsive behaviors: plans/programs
Operationalization: how CSP is measured	personal interview and survey to ascertain information about minority employment, female officers, low income housing loans, minority enterprise loans, donations
FP: nature of financial performance	income, market share, ROA, IBST (income before securities gains or losses and income taxes [they took this and divided it by total assets as a measure of organizational income])
Source of measured financial performance	interviews, *Moody's*, FDIC, Census, *Texas Red Book*
Control variable(s)	local ownership, size of community, federal or state charter, size (assets), managerial values, minority population in the area
Analysis	correlation, ANOVA
General result	+ and 0 and −
Statistical particulars and/or summary of the data analysis	correlations between different measures of CSP and different measures of organizational performance and context vary, but with five different "social behaviors," organizational income has correlation coefficients of .05,.09, .25 (p<.1),-.08, -.28 (p<.1) and corporate market share has correlation coefficients of .31 (p<.1), .24, .06, -.21, -.45 (p<.01)
Strength of results	NA
Authors' recommendations for future research	multi-dimensional approach

Investigator(s)	*Klassen & McLaughlin*
Source and year of publication	*Management Science (1996)*
Sample size (number of companies)	82
Sample type	firms' receiving environmental awards or experiencing environmental crises
Time of observation	1985-91
CSP: nature of corporate social performance investigated	environmental practices
Operationalization: how CSP is measured	environmental awards and crises
FP: nature of financial performance	CAR (cumulative abnormal returns)
Source of measured financial performance	CRSP
Control variable(s)	risk, industry, size, time, award-giver, previous awards
Analysis	event study
General result	+
Statistical particulars and/or summary of the data analysis	awards have a positive impact (.6% to.8%) on market return (p<.01), amounting to a mean of $80.52 million and median of $26.85 million in additional value; crises have a negative effect (-.8% to −1.5%) on market return (p<.05), amounting to a mean of -$390.47 million and a median of -$95.40 in lost value (p. 1208)
Strength of results	moderate
Authors' recommendations for future research	investigate net gain/loss of crisis; improve construct and measurement of environmental performance; quantify the benefits under a variety of circumstances

Investigator(s)	*Klassen and Whybark*
Source and year of publication	*Academy of Management Journal* (1999)
Sample size (number of companies)	66-69
Sample type	furniture industry
Time of observation	1994
CSP: nature of corporate social performance investigated	environmental performance
Operationalization: how CSP is measured	self-reported questionnaire about manufacturing initiatives, coded as pollution control or pollution prevention; Toxic Release Inventory
FP: nature of financial performance	cost, quality, speed, and flexibility of manufacturing operations
Source of measured financial performance	self-reported questionnaire responses
Control variable(s)	size, asset age, manufacturing investment
Analysis	regression
General result	+
Statistical particulars and/or summary of the data analysis	pollution prevention activities reduce cost (b=.909, p<.05) and increase speed (b=1.124, p<.05), flexibility (b=1.006, p<.05), delivery speed (b= -14.737, p<.1), and on-time delivery (b=8.556, p<.05); pollution control, in contrast, increases cost (b= -.716, p<.1) and decreases speed (b= -.853, p<.1), flexibility (b= -.839, p<.1) and on-time delivery (b= -7.014, p<.1); in sum, "As a portfolio [of environmental technologies] was increasingly allocated to pollution prevention technologies, manufacturing performance improved in the areas of cost, speed, and flexibility" (p. 606).
Strength of results	modest
Authors' recommendations for future research	explore the integration of pollution prevention technologies with other strategic resources, examine implementation, and investigate adoption of prevention strategies in related aspects of social performance (e.g., worker safety, disable workers, product liability)

Investigator(s)	*Lashgari and Gant*
Source and year of publication	*Review of Social Economy* (1989)
Sample size (number of companies)	79
Sample type	companies in the top two categories of the Sullivan ratings (for adherence to Sullivan principles in South Africa)
Time of observation	1977-83
CSP: nature of corporate social performance investigated	ethical treatment of employees
Operationalization: how CSP is measured	adherence to Sullivan principles
FP: nature of financial performance	ROI, ROE
Source of measured financial performance	*Compustat*
Control variable(s)	risk
Analysis	ANOVA
General result	0
Statistical particulars and/or summary of the data analysis	**ROE:** Sullivan Category 1 companies ("making good progress") have higher return than Category 2 ("making progress"), which have higher return than the entire stock universe, which has a higher return than the Dow Jones 30 Industrial Average; for risk per unit of return, the stock universe performs best, followed in order by Sullivan Category 2, Sullivan Category 1, and DJIA 30; **ROI:** the entire stock universe has a higher return than Sullivan Category 2, which is higher than Sullivan Category 1, which is higher than the DJIA 30; for risk per unit of return, the stock universe performs best, followed in order by Sullivan Category 1, Sullivan Category 2, and DJIA 30; differences are seldom statistically significant
Strength of results	modest
Authors' recommendations for future research	

Investigator(s)	*Lerner and Fryxell*
Source and year of publication	*Journal of Business Ethics (1988)*
Sample size (number of companies)	113
Sample type	many industries all in report rated by CEP
Time of observation	1979-84
CSP: nature of corporate social performance investigated	(1) CSR, (2) responsiveness, (3) social issues
Operationalization: how CSP is measured	CEP (1986): (1) CSR – charity and disclosure; (2) responsiveness – women and minorities on board and in top management; (3) social issues – involvement in South Africa, military industry involvement, PAC contributions
FP: nature of financial performance	13 variables including ROI, earnings growth, sales growth, market share change
Source of measured financial performance	*Compustat* (1979-84)
Control variable(s)	industry and size (employees)
Analysis	regression
General result	+ and 0 and −
Statistical particulars and/or summary of the data analysis	50 of 117 regression coefficients are significant and 19 of the 50 are size or industry; 7 of 45 relationships between 5 measures of FP and 9 measures of CSP are significant (with either positive or negative coefficients) – 4 negative, 3 positive, 38 are zero; some measures of FP have both positive and negative relationships with the same indicator of CSP
Strength of results	unclear
Authors' recommendations for future research	broader conceptual view of CSP, examinations need more specific measurement of and relationship among variables

Investigator(s)	*Levy and Shatto*
Source and year of publication	*Research in Corporate Social Performance and Policy* (1988)
Sample size (number of companies)	55
Sample type	large electric utilities
Time of observation	1976
CSP: nature of corporate social performance investigated	philanthropic contributions (in health and welfare, education, civics and politics)
Operationalization: how CSP is measured	amount of contributions net income
FP: nature of financial performance	net income
Source of measured financial performance	Form 1 Reports filed with the Federal Energy Administration
Control variable(s)	industry
Analysis	regression
General result	+
Statistical particulars and/or summary of the data analysis	p<.01 for all three domains of charitable giving: they each increase as net income increases
Strength of results	moderate
Authors' recommendations for future research	

Investigator(s)	*Maddox and Siegfried*
Source and year of publication	*Economics of Firm Size, Market Structure, and Social Performance (FTC, 1980)*
Sample size (number of companies)	2,262
Sample type	*IRS Sourcebook of Statistics of Income*
Time of observation	1963 (top p. 216 for explanation: clean year)
CSP: nature of corporate social performance investigated	corporate charitable contributions
Operationalization: how CSP is measured	IRS
FP: nature of financial performance	firm size (sales), industry competition (concentration ratios)
Source of measured financial performance	IRS
Control variable(s)	profits, advertising, R&D
Analysis	regression
General result	+
Statistical particulars and/or summary of the data analysis	size's effect on giving: 1% increase in size = .14% increase in giving (p<.01); market power: p<.1
Strength of results	moderate
Authors' recommendations for future research	study more recent years, impact on charity of additional variables (education level of employees, fraction of output sold directly to consumers, geographic dispersion of plants)

Investigator(s)	*Marcus and Goodman*
Source and year of publication	Research in Corporate Social Performance and Policy (1986)
Sample size (number of companies)	48
Sample type	Allegheny County (Pittsburgh) smokestack industries
Time of observation	1974-77
CSP: nature of corporate social performance investigated	compliance with emissions regulations
Operationalization: how CSP is measured	1977 U.S. EPA report
FP: nature of financial performance	ROA, ROE, debt to equity, long-term debt to equity, capital expenditures to long term debts
Source of measured financial performance	1974-77 annual reports
Control variable(s)	region, extent of the problem (measured as outputs of five emissions), size
Analysis	ANOVA, discriminant analysis
General result	+
Statistical particulars and/or summary of the data analysis	$p < .05$ on 5 of 20 F-statistics
Strength of results	weak
Authors' recommendations for future research	examine specific situation, larger samples and additional years

Investigator(s)	*Marcus and Goodman*
Source and year of publication	Research in Corporate Social Performance and Policy (1986)
Sample size (number of companies)	13
Sample type	nuclear plants
Time of observation	1982
CSP: nature of corporate social performance investigated	conformity with new regulations
Operationalization: how CSP is measured	implementation of Independent Safety Engineering Groups (ISEG) (ascertained from interviews)
FP: nature of financial performance	(1) management capabilities and (2) productive efficiency
Source of measured financial performance	1983 Nuclear Power Safety Report
Control variable(s)	none
Analysis	t-tests
General result	+ and 0
Statistical particulars and/or summary of the data analysis	nuclear plants rated as having a high level of acceptance of ISEG (1) received higher scores on management capability ($p<.0005$); (2) experienced less downtime ($.05<p<.1$)
Strength of results	moderate
Authors' recommendations for future research	examine specific situation, larger samples and additional years

Investigator(s)	*McGuire, Sundgren, and Schneeweis*
Source and year of publication	*Academy of Management Journal (1988)*
Sample size (number of companies)	(1) 98 (2) 131
Sample type	*Fortune Most Admired*
Time of observation	(1)1983-85 (2) 1983
CSP: nature of corporate social performance investigated	reputation for responsibility to the community and environment
Operationalization: how CSP is measured	*Fortune* corporate reputation survey
FP: nature of financial performance	market performance (risk adjusted return [alpha], total return); market risk (beta and standard deviation of total return); accounting performance (ROA, total assets, sales growth, asset growth, operating income growth); accounting risk (debt/assets, operating leverage, standard deviation of operating income)
Source of measured financial performance	*Compustat*
Control variable(s)	risk
Analysis	correlation, regression
General result	+
Statistical particulars and/or summary of the data analysis	adjusted R-squared (p-value for the F): accounting performance – prior .294 (p<.01), subsequent .195 (p<.01); market performance – prior .129 (p<.01), subsequent .052 (p<.05); accounting risk – prior .287 (p<.05), subsequent .193 (p<.01); market risk – prior .211 (p<.01), subsequent .287 (p<.01); note stronger relationships for accounting measures and the "pre" performance measures
Strength of results	moderate
Authors' recommendations for future research	investigate influence of prior firm performance, consider financial performance as a variable influencing social responsibility, and not vice-versa

Investigator(s)	*McWilliams and Siegel*
Source and year of publication	*Strategic Management Journal* (2000)
Sample size (number of companies)	524
Sample type	companies in Domini 400 vs. those that are not
Time of observation	1991-96
CSP: nature of corporate social performance investigated	included in Domini 400 Social Index
Operationalization: how CSP is measured	dummy variable: in or out of DSI 400
FP: nature of financial performance	unspecified
Source of measured financial performance	unspecified
Control variable(s)	firm-level R&D, industry-level advertising intensity
Analysis	correlation, regression
General result	0
Statistical particulars and/or summary of the data analysis	when R&D and advertising intensity are added to the regression equation, the coefficient for CSP ceases to be statistically significant
Strength of results	modest
Authors' recommendations for future research	

Investigator(s)	*Meznar, Nigh, and Kwok*
Source and year of publication	Academy of Management Journal (1994)
Sample size (number of companies)	39
Sample type	companies announcing withdrawal from South Africa
Time of observation	1985-90
CSP: nature of corporate social performance investigated	(1) withdrawal from South Africa and (2) early or late timing of withdrawal
Operationalization: how CSP is measured	press report in one of seven major newspapers
FP: nature of financial performance	CAR (cumulative abnormal return)
Source of measured financial performance	NA
Control variable(s)	other major announcements
Analysis	event study
General result	(1) – (2) early announcements suffered greater stock decrease than later announcements
Statistical particulars and/or summary of the data analysis	(1) negative returns for all nine intervals, and significant at p<.05 or better in 5 of the 9 (strongest impact is from day –20 to 10) (2) 1986 and before = 8% decline in stock price vs. 1987 and after = 2% decline
Strength of results	strong
Authors' recommendations for future research	NA

Investigator(s)	*Moskowitz*
Source and year of publication	*Business and Society Review (1972)*
Sample size (number of companies)	14
Sample type	personal choice (renown)
Time of observation	1972
CSP: nature of corporate social performance investigated	responsiveness to social problems
Operationalization: how CSP is measured	observation of practices, especially toward minorities (board representation, ownership, employees, vendors, product integration), including EEO, but also covering enlightened HR, urban renewal, charity, environment, consumer protection, type of product disclosure, South Africa
FP: nature of financial performance	stock market performance (excess return on funds)
Source of measured financial performance	NA
Control variable(s)	none
Analysis	case studies
General result	+
Statistical particulars and/or summary of the data analysis	mere reported relationship
Strength of results	unclear (editors attached letters cautioning against hasty conclusions)
Authors' recommendations for future research	more research on CSR

Investigator(s)	*Nehrt*
Source and year of publication	*Strategic Management Journal (1996)*
Sample size (number of companies)	50
Sample type	pulp & paper industry
Time of observation	1983-85 and 1989-91
CSP: nature of corporate social performance investigated	environmental practices
Operationalization: how CSP is measured	timing and intensity of investments in pollution-reducing technologies
FP: nature of financial performance	net income growth
Source of measured financial performance	11 sources of firm and industry-specific data, most notably *Pulp & Paper International*
Control variable(s)	timing of regulations, GDP growth, real wages growth, initial net income, sales growth
Analysis	regression (OLS)
General result	+
Statistical particulars and/or summary of the data analysis	timing of investments has a positive impact on financial performance (p<.05), and intensity alone has a negative effect (p<.05 in the model with outliers removed); early movers have a distinct advantage, especially if they invest a great deal
Strength of results	moderate
Authors' recommendations for future research	NA

Investigator(s)	*Newgren, Rasher, LaRoe, and Szabo*
Source and year of publication	Research in Corporate Social Performance and Policy (1985)
Sample size (number of companies)	50
Sample type	largest firms in five industrial and five non-industrial classifications
Time of observation	1975-80
CSP: nature of corporate social performance investigated	environmental assessment (environment meaning external context; other terms for environmental assessment include sociopolitical forecasting, social forecasting, or noneconomic forecasting)
Operationalization: how CSP is measured	questionnaires (then coded for the degree of environmental assessment)
FP: nature of financial performance	market performance (industry-adjusted price-earnings ratio)
Source of measured financial performance	*Value Line* investment survey
Control variable(s)	industrial vs. non-industrial firms
Analysis	ANOVA, analysis of variance and covariance including repeated measures
General result	+
Statistical particulars and/or summary of the data analysis	companies performing environmental assessment outperformed companies not practicing environmental assessment (p<.05)
Strength of results	moderate
Authors' recommendations for future research	personal aspirations and technical developments as variables

Investigator(s)	*Ogden and Watson*
Source and year of publication	*Academy of Management Journal (1999)*
Sample size (number of companies)	10
Sample type	privatized water companies in U.K.
Time of observation	1991-97
CSP: nature of corporate social performance investigated	customer service
Operationalization: how CSP is measured	complaints to Office of Water Services (OFWAT) and annual reports filed by companies with OFWAT reporting incidents of: inadequate water pressure, supply interruptions, responses to billing queries, responses to written complaints
FP: nature of financial performance	(1) profitability and (2) shareholder wealth
Source of measured financial performance	(1) sector-relative profit: [profits/equity] – [sector-average profits/equity], (2) industry adjusted returns: firm [returns] – [sector-average returns]
Control variable(s)	"firm level fixed-effects" (idiosyncratic characteristics of each company: pricing regulations, inherited infrastructure, location-specific costs, limited scope for increasing sales)
Analysis	regression
General result	(1) – for profitability and (2) 0 for shareholder wealth
Statistical particulars and/or summary of the data analysis	(1) $p<.01$ and (2) positive but non-significant: as predicted, firms invest to take care of customers but no statistical evidence indicates that shareholders alter their expectations about the value of the firm
Strength of results	strong
Authors' recommendations for future research	NA

Investigator(s)	*O'Neill, Saunders, and McCarthy*
Source and year of publication	*Journal of Business Ethics (1989)*
Sample size (number of companies)	140 companies (157 respondents out of 840 possible)
Sample type	*Fortune Most Admired*
Time of observation	NA
CSP: nature of corporate social performance investigated	board members' concern for corporate social responsibility
Operationalization: how CSP is measured	survey (19.6% net usable rate; 23% response rate)
FP: nature of financial performance	ROA (five-year and one-year) and risk-adjusted ROA
Source of measured financial performance	*Compustat* and *Value Line*
Control variable(s)	risk
Analysis	correlation
General result	0
Statistical particulars and/or summary of the data analysis	non-significant correlations between concern for society and all financial performance measures (short and long-term ROA and short and long-term risk-adjusted ROA)
Strength of results	weak
Authors' recommendations for future research	NA

Investigator(s)	*Parket and Eilbirt*
Source and year of publication	*Business Horizons (1975)*
Sample size (number of companies)	80 vs. the other 420 in the *Fortune 500*
Sample type	respondents (from *Forbes* directory) to CSR survey vs. *Fortune 500* (without *Forbes* respondents)
Time of observation	1973
CSP: nature of corporate social performance investigated	education/art, ecology, minority training/hiring
Operationalization: how CSP is measured	those who responded to prior survey about CSR (survey using a more/less dummy variable)
FP: nature of financial performance	net income, profit margin, ROE, EPS
Source of measured financial performance	*Fortune 500*
Control variable(s)	none
Analysis	mere reported relationship: median profit comparisons in the two groups of companies
General result	+
Statistical particulars and/or summary of the data analysis	no statistical tests, companies of the 80 respondents (indicator of concern for CSR) seemed to outperform the non-respondent companies
Strength of results	weak
Authors' recommendations for future research	"discover how programs of this sort come to be initiated" (p. 10)

Investigator(s)	*Patten*
Source and year of publication	*Accounting, Organizations and Society (1990)*
Sample size (number of companies)	37
Sample type	U.S. Companies
Time of observation	1977
CSP: nature of corporate social performance investigated	signing Sullivan principles
Operationalization: how CSP is measured	announcement of adoption of Sullivan principles
FP: nature of financial performance	mean abnormal returns and trading volume
Source of measured financial performance	*S&P Daily Stock Price Record*
Control variable(s)	industry, size (revenues, capitalization)
Analysis	7-day matched-pair event study
General result	0
Statistical particulars and/or summary of the data analysis	no difference in return but trading volume increased prior to announcement for companies NOT signing Sullivan principles (the presumption was that all companies would sign the principles)
Strength of results	weak, few effects in the traditional event window
Authors' recommendations for future research	discover how and why disclosed information is used and then how it can be best provided

Investigator(s)	*Patten*
Source and year of publication	*Journal of Accounting and Public Policy (1991)*
Sample size (number of companies)	128 (47 "high" and 81 "low")
Sample type	*Fortune 500*
Time of observation	1985
CSP: nature of corporate social performance investigated	disclosure
Operationalization: how CSP is measured	companies coded as "high" (greater than or equal to one-quarter of a page) or "low" (less than one-tenth of a page) based on annual report disclosures of: environment, energy, fair business practices, human resources, community involvement, products, other disclosures
FP: nature of financial performance	ROA, ROE
Source of measured financial performance	1984 and 1985 *Fortune 500* report and *Value Line* reports
Control variable(s)	size, industry
Analysis	regression
General result	0
Statistical particulars and/or summary of the data analysis	all measures of ROE and ROA are non-significant; size ($p<.001$) and industry ($p<.01$) are significantly related to disclosure
Strength of results	strong
Authors' recommendations for future research	use "less noisy proxies for public pressure" (p. 305)

Investigator(s)	*Pava and Krausz*
Source and year of publication	*Journal of Business Ethics (1996)*
Sample size (number of companies)	53 in response group, 53 in control group
Sample type	sample identified by CEP vs. matched pairs not identified by CEP
Time of observation	1985-87, 1989-91
CSP: nature of corporate social performance investigated	social reputation
Operationalization: how CSP is measured	CEP rating of 12 components
FP: nature of financial performance	market (market return, price/earnings, market/book); accounting (ROA, ROA, EPS); risk (debt/equity, interest coverage, Altman's Z [bankruptcy likelihood]); other: capital investment, size, # of lines of business, dividend payout ratio
Source of measured financial performance	*Compustat*
Control variable(s)	matched sample
Analysis	t-test
General result	0 to +
Statistical particulars and/or summary of the data analysis	Market: higher mean return over 7 years (meaningless); higher 4 of 7 years; $p<.1$ for CSPers>Non-CSPers in 1986 & Non-CSPers>CSPers in 1988; price/earnings show no difference except in 1990 ($p<.1$ for CSPers>Non-CSPers); Accounting: ROA (CSPers>Non-CSPers except in one year; significant in two), EPS (no difference), ROE (no difference); Risk: beta (risk) is greater for CSPers in 3 years at $p<.1$ but debt/equity, Altman's Z, interest coverage, liquidity ratios all show no difference; Time: inconclusive. Total tally: 15 of 98 t-tests on performance variables show significant differences, with 14 of the 15 revealing better performance for the CSP firms than for the non-CSP firms. 8 of the 12 are significant at $p<.05$, the rest at $p<.1$. However, with 98 tests and $p<.1$, you would expect 10 of the results to be significant by chance alone
Strength of results	none to minimal difference in financial performance (therefore no cost to CSP or no evidence that CSP hurts financial performance)
Authors' recommendations for future research	more empirical studies linking CSP to financial performance; role of CEO in establishing CSR goals; how corporations defend and justify CSR expenditures in their annual report

Investigator(s)	*Porter and van der Linde*
Source and year of publication	*Harvard Business Review (1995)*
Sample size (number of companies)	181
Sample type	chemical companies
Time of observation	1991-94
CSP: nature of corporate social performance investigated	environmental practices
Operationalization: how CSP is measured	waste prevention
FP: nature of financial performance	cost increases and reductions
Source of measured financial performance	company reported data
Control variable(s)	industry
Analysis	mere reported relationship
General result	+
Statistical particulars and/or summary of the data analysis	of 181 waste prevention activities, only 1 resulted in a net cost increase (p. 125);$3.49 average annual savings per dollar spent on source reduction for 27 activities (p.125); provides case exemplars from Rhone-Poulenc, Thermo Electron, Dow, 3M, Du Pont, Ciba-Geigy, Cummins Engine, Dutch flower industry
Strength of results	unclear
Authors' recommendations for future research	NA

Investigator(s)	*Posnikoff*
Source and year of publication	Contemporary Economic Policy (1997)
Sample size (number of companies)	40
Sample type	companies announcing withdrawal from South Africa
Time of observation	1980-91
CSP: nature of corporate social performance investigated	disinvestment from South Africa
Operationalization: how CSP is measured	reports in New York Times and Wall Street Journal
FP: nature of financial performance	abnormal returns [(1) comparison period returns, (2) market-adjusted returns, (3) comparison to OLS market-predicted returns
Source of measured financial performance	CRSP
Control variable(s)	comparison period, market return, risk
Analysis	event study
General result	+
Statistical particulars and/or summary of the data analysis	for the event period comprising one day before, the day of, and the day after announcement of disinvestment, as well as for the period comprising one day before and the day of disinvestment, all three methods of calculating abnormal returns render results that range from $p<.01$ to $p<.1$. Of 14 test statistics, 10 are statistically significant at $p<.1$ or better, and 5 of those are statistically significant at $p<.05$
Strength of results	moderate
Authors' recommendations for future research	

Investigator(s)	*Preston*
Source and year of publication	*Journal of Contemporary Business (1978)*
Sample size (number of companies)	97
Sample type	*Fortune 500*
Time of observation	1971-75
CSP: nature of corporate social performance investigated	disclosure in annual report
Operationalization: how CSP is measured	pages of social performance disclosure in annual report
FP: nature of financial performance	ROE
Source of measured financial performance	NA
Control variable(s)	none
Analysis	mere reported relationship
General result	+
Statistical particulars and/or summary of the data analysis	14.5% median ROE for 71 "high-reporting" firms compared to a median of 11.6% for entire Fortune 500 and 12.5% for 26 "non-reporting" firms; no statistical test (pp. 147-148)
Strength of results	unclear
Authors' recommendations for future research	standardize CSR reporting format

Investigator(s)	*Preston and O'Bannon*
Source and year of publication	*Business & Society (1997)*
Sample size (number of companies)	67
Sample type	*Fortune Most Admired*
Time of observation	1982-92
CSP: nature of corporate social performance investigated	corporate reputation (3 attributes reflecting 3 stakeholders)
Operationalization: how CSP is measured	3 attributes from *Fortune* corporate reputation study (attributes: responsibility to the community and environment; select and retain good people; quality or products and services)
FP: nature of financial performance	ROE, ROA, ROI
Source of measured financial performance	*Compustat*
Control variable(s)	none
Analysis	correlation (contemporaneous and lead-lag)
General result	+
Statistical particulars and/or summary of the data analysis	270 correlations, no negative social-financial performance correlations; only 8 of 93 correlations between CSP and ROA are non-significant
Strength of results	strong
Authors' recommendations for future research	NA

Investigator(s)	*Preston and Sapienza*
Source and year of publication	*Journal of Behavioral Economics (1990)*
Sample size (number of companies)	108
Sample type	*Fortune Most Admired*
Time of observation	1982-1986
CSP: nature of corporate social performance investigated	stakeholder reputation ratings (6 attributes)
Operationalization: how CSP is measured	*Fortune* corporate reputation study (shareholders – 3 attributes; employees – 1 attribute; customers – 1 attribute; community – 1 attribute)
FP: nature of financial performance	(1) size, (2) growth, (3) profitability
Source of measured financial performance	*Fortune*: (1) 1986 sales volume, (2) % increase in sales, 1982-86, (3) 10-year total rate of return
Control variable(s)	industry
Analysis	correlation
General result	+
Statistical particulars and/or summary of the data analysis	correlation coefficients range from .04 (between 5-year growth and responsibility to community and environment, n.s.) to .49 (between 10-year rate of return and reputation for financial performance, p<.01); 7 of 9 correlation coefficients for three *Fortune* attributes (product, people, and community) are positive
Strength of results	moderate
Authors' recommendations for future research	NA

Investigator(s)	*Rockness, Schlachter, and Rockness*
Source and year of publication	*Advances in Public Interest Accounting (1986)*
Sample size (number of companies)	21
Sample type	chemical industry
Time of observation	1969 and 1979
CSP: nature of corporate social performance investigated	hazardous waste
Operationalization: how CSP is measured	EPA Superfund National Priorities List, U.S. House of Representatives Site Survey
FP: nature of financial performance	ROE, ROA, ROS, excess market value, asset turnover, financial solvency; asset age and asset size (used as performance and controls)
Source of measured financial performance	*Compustat*
Control variable(s)	industry, size, age
Analysis	Spearman rank correlation
General result	0
Statistical particulars and/or summary of the data analysis	only ROE associated with smaller on-site waste disposal $p<.1$; of 92 correlations, 12 are significant at $p<.1$ and 4 at $p<.5$ or $p<.01$: 4 of the significant correlations are positive and 12 are negative
Strength of results	weak
Authors' recommendations for future research	refinement in measurement of the hazardous waste disposal variables

Investigator(s)	*Russo and Fouts*
Source and year of publication	*Academy of Management Journal (1997)*
Sample size (number of companies)	243
Sample type	Franklin Research and Development Corporation (FRDC)
Time of observation	1991-92
CSP: nature of corporate social performance investigated	environmental behavior (compliance and prevention)
Operationalization: how CSP is measured	FRDC's ratings, transformed into a 1 to 5 scale
FP: nature of financial performance	ROA
Source of measured financial performance	*Compustat*
Control variable(s)	industry growth rate, industry concentration, firm growth rate, firm size (sales), advertising intensity, precise role of consumption behavior in the equation
Analysis	regression
General result	+
Statistical particulars and/or summary of the data analysis	for pooled data (1991 & 92): coefficient for environmental rating = 1.49 (p<.01); change in R-squared of .01 (p<.01); For 1991: n.s.; For 1992: 1.60 (p<.05), change in R-squared of .01 (4.28)
Strength of results	moderate: robust, yet modest results — they may be statistically significant but perhaps not practically significant (e.g., a change in R-squared of .01 is significant at .01)
Authors' recommendations for future research	identify full chain of variables connecting environmental performance to financial performance, before and after studies of pro-environment changes; boundary conditions (where do returns to environmental performance stop?); longitudinal research

Investigator(s)	*Shane and Spicer*
Source and year of publication	The Accounting Review (1983)
Sample size (number of companies)	58 (full inclusion of 58 out of sample of 72)
Sample type	4 major pollution producing industries
Time of observation	1970-75
CSP: nature of corporate social performance investigated	air and water pollution measures
Operationalization: how CSP is measured	CEP
FP: nature of financial performance	mean adjusted returns
Source of measured financial performance	CRSP tapes
Control variable(s)	industry
Analysis	event study
General result	+
Statistical particulars and/or summary of the data analysis	abnormal returns (price decrease) −2 and −1 days before CEP report; poor pollution control companies had negative returns on day of newspaper report day (0) compared to good performers
Strength of results	modest
Authors' recommendations for future research	examine social accounting information, understand how market forms expectations, learn how to separate regulation effects from disclosure

Investigator(s)	*Sharma and Vredenburg*
Source and year of publication	*Strategic Management Journal* (1998)
Sample size (number of companies)	99
Sample type	Canadian oil and gas companies
Time of observation	1996
CSP: nature of corporate social performance investigated	environmental strategy
Operationalization: how CSP is measured	survey responses
FP: nature of financial performance	intermediate benefits
Source of measured financial performance	survey response about cost reduction, improved operations and management practices, product quality, employee morale, corporate reputation and goodwill, fast regulatory approvals, product differentiation, improved ability to compete in the future
Control variable(s)	industry
Analysis	bivariate regression
General result	+
Statistical particulars and/or summary of the data analysis	organizational capabilities is driven by environmental strategy (b=.4569 for environmental strategy, $p < .0001$), and benefits to the firm are in turn driven by organizational capabilities (b=.7207 for capabilities, $p < .0001$)
Strength of results	moderate
Authors' recommendations for future research	identify which specific organizational capabilities produce which benefits

Investigator(s)	*Simerly*
Source and year of publication	*Psychological Reports (1995)*
Sample size (number of companies)	84: 42 pairs of companies in 42 manufacturing industries
Sample type	*Fortune Most Admired*
Time of observation	1988-90
CSP: nature of corporate social performance investigated	responsiveness to community and environment (high and low groups)
Operationalization: how CSP is measured	the one *Fortune* corporate reputation survey criterion on responsibility to community and environment (firms that were one standard deviation above and below the mean)
FP: nature of financial performance	average ROE for 1988-90
Source of measured financial performance	annual reports
Control variable(s)	amount of stock held by the top manager, debt/equity (measure of risk)
Analysis	regression
General result	+
Statistical particulars and/or summary of the data analysis	.392 (p<.01) for ROE as predictor of CSP for the group of companies highly rated on CSP
Strength of results	strong
Authors' recommendations for future research	NA

Investigator(s)	*Spencer and Taylor*
Source and year of publication	*Akron Business and Economic Review (1987)*
Sample size (number of companies)	120
Sample type	*Fortune Most Admired*
Time of observation	1977-82
CSP: nature of corporate social performance investigated	responsibility to community and environment
Operationalization: how CSP is measured	*Fortune* corporate reputation survey (one of the eight attributes)
FP: nature of financial performance	ROA, ROS
Source of measured financial performance	*Fortune*
Control variable(s)	industry
Analysis	"within and between analysis" (intraclass correlation)
General result	+
Statistical particulars and/or summary of the data analysis	relationship exists at the industry level
Strength of results	modest
Authors' recommendations for future research	address question of causality, better measure of CSP, do industry studies

Investigator(s)	*Spicer*
Source and year of publication	*The Accounting Review (1978)* [NOTE: these same data are analyzed from the perspective of risk, without a specific examination of CSP-FP link, in Spicer's *Journal of Business Finance and Accounting* article, 1978.]
Sample size (number of companies)	18
Sample type	pulp & paper industry
Time of observation	1968-73, 1969-71, 1971-73
CSP: nature of corporate social performance investigated	pollution control
Operationalization: how CSP is measured	pollution control indices based on information from CEP
FP: nature of financial performance	profit, size, total/systematic risk, price/earnings
Source of measured financial performance	*Compustat*
Control variable(s)	industry
Analysis	Spearman rank correlation, Mann-Whitney U
General result	+
Statistical particulars and/or summary of the data analysis	8 of 14 tests for significance are significant at $p<.05$: Spearman correlation coefficients for profitability and 4 pollution indices: .2484 (n.s.), .3287 ($p<.1$), .4526 ($p<.05$), .5551 ($p<.05$); Mann-Whitney U for profitability and 4 pollution indices: 12 ($p<.1$); 13, ($p<.05$), 13, ($p<.1$), 10 ($p<.05$); Spearman correlation coefficients for price/earnings ratio and 4 pollution indices: .6839 ($p<.001$), .6353 ($p<.01$), .1255 (n.s.), .2078 (n.s.); Mann-Whitney U for price/earnings ratio and 4 pollution indices: 5 ($p<.01$), 16 ($p<.1$), 5 ($p<.01$), 15 (n.s.)
Strength of results	modest
Authors' recommendations for future research	extend study to other industries

Investigator(s)	*Stevens*
Source and year of publication	*Advances in Accounting (1984)*
Sample size (number of companies)	48
Sample type	CEP (pulp & paper, petroleum, steel, electrical utilities)
Time of observation	1972-77
CSP: nature of corporate social performance investigated	environmental practices
Operationalization: how CSP is measured	CEP estimates of pollution abatement costs
FP: nature of financial performance	excess market return (monthly, cumulative, average)
Source of measured financial performance	CRSP
Control variable(s)	risk, companies without pollution abatement problems
Analysis	event study
General result	+
Statistical particulars and/or summary of the data analysis	a portfolio of companies with high pollution abatement estimates suffers a mean decrease in value relative to a control portfolio and relative to a portfolio of companies with low pollution abatement estimates (p<.1 for both)
Strength of results	moderate
Authors' recommendations for future research	investigate how investors use environmental data; investigate the information content of other measures of environmental performance; compare CEP data to firm data to assess accuracy, reliability, and relevance

Investigator(s)	*Sturdivant and Ginter*
Source and year of publication	*California Management Review (1977)*
Sample size (number of companies)	28
Sample type	Moskowitz's 67 companies
Time of observation	1964-74
CSP: nature of corporate social performance investigated	social responsiveness
Operationalization: how CSP is measured	Moskowitz's rating: best, honorable mention, worst
FP: nature of financial performance	earnings per share growth
Source of measured financial performance	*Fortune*
Control variable(s)	industry
Analysis	t-tests
General result	+
Statistical particulars and/or summary of the data analysis	p<.01 for best CSR and honorable mention CSR each outperforming worst, relative to industry (EPS growth vs. industry – best: 1.18; honorable mention: 1.26; worst: .69)
Strength of results	modest
Authors' recommendations for future research	NA

Investigator(s)	*Teoh, Welch, and Wazzan*
Source and year of publication	*Journal of Business (1999)*
Sample size (number of companies)	(1) 9 banks; (2) 16 pension funds; (3) 46 firms
Sample type	banks with South African loans; pension funds divesting; firms voluntarily divesting
Time of observation	1985-88
CSP: nature of corporate social performance investigated	divestment from South Africa
Operationalization: how CSP is measured	divestment announcements and legislative activity leading up to passage of the Comprehensive Anti-Apartheid Act of 1986 (Investor Responsibility Research Center, Dow Jones News Retrieval, *Wall Street Journal*)
FP: nature of financial performance	abnormal market returns
Source of measured financial performance	CRSP, *Financial Times*
Control variable(s)	sales, assets, employees
Analysis	event study
General result	0
Statistical particulars and/or summary of the data analysis	a "detectable (but small) change in the composition of shareholders" following a divestment announcement (p. 73): number of institutional shareholders increased by 1.2% (p<.1) in the divestment announcement month; percent of shares held by institutional investors increased by 20% (p<.1) in the divestment month. Other than these findings, there is scarce statistically significant evidence of any financial impact of U.S. legislation or divestment decisions. The Comprehensive Anti-Apartheid Act of 1986 did not have a significant impact on the U.S. banking sector (p. 58) or the South African financial markets (p. 62); divestment announcements by pension funds did not significantly hurt firms with major South African operations (p. 68); voluntary divestment announcements of corporations with operations in South Africa had neither positive nor negative financial effects (p. 77); firms with operations in South African that were hit with sanctions and legislative actions did not perform unusually poorly in the 1980s (p. 79)
Strength of results	strong
Authors' recommendations for future research	NA

Investigator(s)	*Tichy, McGill, and St. Clair*
Source and year of publication	*Corporate Global Citizenship: Doing Business in the Public Eye (1997)*
Sample size (number of companies)	10
Sample type	*Fortune Most Admired*
Time of observation	12/31/82-12/31/96
CSP: nature of corporate social performance investigated	responsibility to the community and environment
Operationalization: how CSP is measured	ranked in the top three on *Fortune's* corporate reputation survey item about community and environmental responsibility
FP: nature of financial performance	total ROE from 12/31/82-12/31/96
Source of measured financial performance	Standard & Poor's
Control variable(s)	industry ROE (S&P measure)
Analysis	no statistical analysis
General result	+: companies ranking in top three on community/environment item far outpace the relevant industry average ROE
Statistical particulars and/or summary of the data analysis	average ROE for firms in sample of 1143% (vs. 742% for S&P 500); average difference between firms in sample and their relevant industry: 882%
Strength of results	NA (compelling picture absent a statistical test)
Authors' recommendations for future research	NA

PERFORMANCE

Investigator(s)	*Vance*
Source and year of publication	Management Review (1975)
Sample size (number of companies)	(1) 14 and (2) 45
Sample type	(1) Moskowitz's sample and (2) major corporations rated in Business & Society Review survey
Time of observation	1972-75
CSP: nature of corporate social performance investigated	social responsibility
Operationalization: how CSP is measured	Moskowitz's recommendations and survey ratings in Business and Society Review
FP: nature of financial performance	percentage change in stock price
Source of measured financial performance	NA
Control variable(s)	none
Analysis	regression (OLS for the 45-firm sample)
General result	−
Statistical particulars and/or summary of the data analysis	coefficients of −23 and −18
Strength of results	strong but generally meaningless ("But companies have more reasons to be socially responsible than only how it affects the per share value of their common stock" [p. 24].)
Authors' recommendations for future research	NA

Investigator(s)	*Verschoor*
Source and year of publication	*Journal of Business Ethics (1998)*
Sample size (number of companies)	376
Sample type	*1997 Business Week 1000*
Time of observation	1996-97
CSP: nature of corporate social performance investigated	a stated commitment (in the annual report) to ethical behavior
Operationalization: how CSP is measured	1996 annual reports
FP: nature of financial performance	total return (1 and 3 year), profit growth (1 and 3 year), sales growth (1 and 3 year), net margin, and ROE
Source of measured financial performance	*Business Week 1000 (1997)*
Control variable(s)	none
Analysis	Mann-Whitney U
General result	+
Statistical particulars and/or summary of the data analysis	compared mean financial rank of those with a stated commitment to ethics against those without
Strength of results	p<.01
Authors' recommendations for future research	NA

Investigator(s)	*Waddock and Graves*
Source and year of publication	*Strategic Management Journal (1997)*
Sample size (number of companies)	469
Sample type	S&P 500
Time of observation	1989-90
CSP: nature of corporate social performance investigated	social performance
Operationalization: how CSP is measured	KLD ratings (community, employees, environment, products, women & minorities, military, nuclear, South Africa)
FP: nature of financial performance	ROA, ROE, ROS,
Source of measured financial performance	*Compustat*
Control variable(s)	size (total sales, total assets, employees), risk (debt/total assets), industry
Analysis	lagged regression
General result	+ (both directions)
Statistical particulars and/or summary of the data analysis	CSP regressed on Financial Performance: ROA p<.001; ROE p<.1, ROS, p<.05; Financial Performance regressed on CSP: ROA p<.01; ROE n.s.; ROS p<.05
Strength of results	strong
Authors' recommendations for future research	examine lags other than 1 year, examine if relationship holds over time, control for the quality of management, alter definitions of CSP to align them with stakeholder relations

Investigator(s)	*Waddock, Graves, and Gorski*
Source and year of publication	*Journal of Investing* (forthcoming)
Sample size (number of companies)	500
Sample type	S&P 500
Time of observation	1996
CSP: nature of corporate social performance investigated	product, employee relations, diversity, community relations, environment, non-US operations, other
Operationalization: how CSP is measured	KLD
FP: nature of financial performance	accounting: ROA, ROE, debt/assets; market: total return to shareholders (for ten, five, and three year)
Source of measured financial performance	*Compustat*
Control variable(s)	size
Analysis	t-test
General result	0
Statistical particulars and/or summary of the data analysis	S&P 500 companies that made it into the DSI 400 (KLD's socially responsible index fund) have better ratings on six of the seven positive social performance screens than S&P 500 companies that did not make it into the DSI 400; those that are in the DSI 400 also out-performed the non-DSI 400 companies on all measures of financial performance except debt/assets, though none of the differences was statistically significant ("there are no notable performance penalties for investing in the group deemed more socially responsible," p. 17)
Strength of results	moderate
Authors' recommendations for future research	

Investigator(s)	*Wokutch and Spencer*
Source and year of publication	*California Management Review (1987)*
Sample size (number of companies)	111 (trimmed to 74 for ANOVA)
Sample type	manufacturing companies in *Fortune Most Admired*
Time of observation	1978-82
CSP: nature of corporate social performance investigated	(1) corporate reputation, (2) crime, (3) philanthropy
Operationalization: how CSP is measured	(1) "responsibility to the community/environment" attribute of the *Fortune* corporate reputation study, (2) 1980-83 issues of Trade Cases (lists litigation) (3) *The Corporate 500: The Directory of Corporate Philanthropy*
FP: nature of financial performance	average 5-year (1978-82) ROA and ROS
Source of measured financial performance	*Fortune 500*
Control variable(s)	type of firm (manufacturing)
Analysis	ANOVA
General result	+
Statistical particulars and/or summary of the data analysis	companies with both low philanthropy and high crime have a lower *Fortune* CSR rating and lower ROA and ROS (significance level not given); philanthropy appears to be more important in *Fortune*'s measure of CSR than does crime (the high crime, high philanthropy category also had a low *Fortune* rating)
Strength of results	weak
Authors' recommendations for future research	concrete measure of CSR, other categories of corporate crime (physical damage, high publicity cases) more diverse sample, use time series data

Investigator(s)	*Wright and Ferris*
Source and year of publication	*Strategic Management Journal (1997)*
Sample size (number of companies)	31
Sample type	companies (with good ratings on Sullivan principles) announcing withdrawal from South Africa
Time of observation	1984-90
CSP: nature of corporate social performance investigated	divestment from South Africa
Operationalization: how CSP is measured	reports in *New York Times* and *Wall Street Journal*
FP: nature of financial performance	mean excess return
Source of measured financial performance	CRSP
Control variable(s)	NA
Analysis	event study
General result	-
Statistical particulars and/or summary of the data analysis	"on the event day, there is a statistically significant negative excess return of -.249 percent" (p.81), at $p<.05$; that is the only day on which there is a statistically significant excess return
Strength of results	moderate
Authors' recommendations for future research	

DISCLOSURE:
4 Studies

Investigator(s)	*Belkaoui and Karpik*
Source and year of publication	*Accounting, Auditing and Accountability Journal (1989)*
Sample size (companies)	23
Sample type	*Business and Society Review*
Time of observation	1973
Predictors of disclosure	(1)social performance, (2)economic performance, (3)monitoring and contracting costs, (4)political visibility
Operationalization: how predictors are measured	(1) reputation (1972 *Business and Society Review* rankings) (2a) NITA (ROA) and (2b) five-year stock return, (3a) leverage, (3b) dividends/unrestricted retained earnings (4a) size (4b) risk (beta) (4c) capital intensive ratio (fixed assets/sales)
Outcome variable(s)	disclosure
Operationalization: how outcome variable is measured	number of social programs disclosed (Ernst & Ernst social disclosure survey)
Control variable(s)	none other than those in equation
Analysis	regression
General result	+ and 0 for CSP-FP link; for tested relationships (1) +, (2a) 0, (2b) 0, (3a) +, (3b) 0, (4a) +, (4b) +, (4c) 0
Statistical particulars and/or summary of the data analysis	correlation between social performance measure and NITA (ROA) is -.3558; correlation between social performance measure and stock return is .2248
Strength of results	strong, but small sample
Authors' recommendations for future research	more research on determinants disclosure, better measure for CSR, use less politically visible companies

DISCLOSURE

Investigator(s)	*Cowen, Ferreri, and Parker*
Source and year of publication	*Accounting, Organizations and Society (1987)*
Sample size (companies)	134
Sample type	*Fortune 500* (data taken from Ernst & Whinney's 1978 survey on CSR disclosure)
Time of observation	size and CSR: 1978; ROE: 1976-78
Predictors of disclosure	*Fortune* rank, ROE, Social Responsibility Committee
Operationalization: how predictors are measured	ROE (*Value Line*)
Outcome variable(s)	corporate social responsibility disclosures
Operationalization: how outcome variable is measured	8 types of disclosure from Ernst & Whinney's survey of annual reports (environment, energy, fair business practices, human resources, community, products, other)
Control variable(s)	size, industry
Analysis	regression
General result	0
Statistical particulars and/or summary of the data analysis	ROE has a non-significant relationship with total disclosure (p=.55); chemical companies disclose more; size and industry affect likelihood of certain types of disclosure; total disclosure = p<.001 for size; size is the most significant explanatory variable; chemical industry differs from others
Strength of results	modest
Authors' recommendations for future research	are corporate social responsibility disclosures correlated with degree of actual corporate social concern?

131

Investigator(s)	*Mills and Gardner*
Source and year of publication	*Journal of Business Research (1984)*
Sample size (companies)	1976: 172 disclosing and 241 not; 1977: 165 disclosing and 252 not
Sample type	*Fortune 500*
Time of observation	1976-77
Predictors of disclosure	capital turnover, leverage, liquidity, ROA, ROI, ROE, 4 measures of return to shareholders
Operationalization: how predictors are measured	*Compustat*
Outcome variable(s)	disclosure of monetary expenditures on socially responsible activities
Operationalization: how outcome variable is measured	Ernst & Whinney survey of annual reports
Control variable(s)	size, firm growth rate
Analysis	discriminant analysis
General result	+
Statistical particulars and/or summary of the data analysis	discriminant analysis does not analyze relationship between disclosure and individual financial terms
Strength of results	more likely to disclose CSR if financial profile is good
Authors' recommendations for future research	more firms with extended time period, investors' perceptions of CSR expenditures on their wealth, market reaction to disclosures

Investigator(s)	*Roberts*
Source and year of publication	*Accounting, Organizations and Society (1992)*
Sample size (companies)	80
Sample type	CEP (1986)
Time of observation	1984-86
Predictors of disclosure	(1) stakeholder power, (2) strategic posture, (3) economic performance
Operationalization: how predictors are measured	(1a) owners with more than 5%, (1b) PAC contributions (CEP), (1c) debt/equity (*Compustat*), (2a) number of public affairs employees (*National Directory of Corporate Public Affairs*), (2b) philanthropic foundation (*National Directory of Corporate Public Affairs*), (3a) Annual change in ROE (*Compustat*), (3b) Beta (*Compustat*) -- our focus is on (3a) in particular, but (3b) as well
Outcome variable(s)	level of disclosure
Operationalization: how outcome variable is measured	CEP
Control variable(s)	age, size, industry, leverage
Analysis	regression (logistic and OLS)
General result	+
Statistical particulars and/or summary of the data analysis	(1a) n.s., (1b) p<.05, (1c) p<.1, (2a) p<.1, (2b) p<.01, (3a) p<.05, (3b) p<.1
Strength of results	modest
Authors' recommendations for future research	influence of other types of stakeholders on disclosure, replicate study using direct measures of CSR as dependent variable

REPUTATION:
3 Studies

Investigator(s)	*Brown and Perry*
Source and year of publication	*Academy of Management Journal (1994)*
Sample size (number of companies)	234
Sample type	*Fortune Most Admired*
Time of observation	1991 ratings, 1988-91 financial data
Predictors of reputation	financial performance: ROA, relative market/book value, log of sales, growth, risk
Operationalization: how predictors are measured	*Compustat*
Outcome variable(s)	reputation
Operationalization: how outcome variable is measured	8 attributes in *Fortune* corporate reputation survey
Control variable(s)	risk
Analysis	regression
General result	+
Statistical particulars and/or summary of the data analysis	R-squared (regressing each of the 8 *Fortune* attributes on the five financial measures) ranged from .36 to .59; for the *Fortune* item, "responsibility to the community and environment," the coefficients for four of five financial indicators (ROA, relative market to book value, sales, and risk) were significant at $p<.001$ and R-squared was .41; the authors use these equations to create a "halo index" for deflating the *Fortune* attributes; but those regressions could be read (contrary to the authors' intent, but consistent with others' interpretations [e.g., Simerly, 1999; Szwajkowski & Figlewicz, 1997]) as evidence of a CSP-FP link
Strength of results	strong (validated three ways) evidence that *Fortune* ratings have financial halo; moderate for CSP-FP relationships
Authors' recommendations for future research	adjust for halo when using *Fortune* corporate reputation index

Investigator(s)	*Fombrun and Shanley*
Source and year of publication	*Academy of Management Journal (1990)*
Sample size (number of companies)	269 (157 for CSR)
Sample type	*Fortune 500*
Time of observation	1985
Predictors of reputation	philanthropic contributions and foundations
Operationalization: how predictors are measured	*(1) Taft Corporate Giving Directory, (2) Corporate Foundation Profiles, (3) Corporate 500: Directory of Corporate Philanthropy, 1986, (4) The Foundation Directory* (1985)
Outcome variable(s)	social reputation
Operationalization: how outcome variable is measured	*Fortune* corporate reputation survey (alpha of all 8 attributes = .97) , *Compustat*, O'Neill Data Graphs
Control variable(s)	normalization by sector; diversification
Analysis	time series regression
General result	+
Statistical particulars and/or summary of the data analysis	no diversification in model: .10 (p<.1) for charity, .15 (p<.01) for foundations; diversification in the model: .07 for charity (n.s.), .13 (p<.05) for foundations
Strength of results	moderate
Authors' recommendations for future research	specify the particular interpretive process through which firms' investments become cognitions in others' minds

Investigator(s)	*McGuire, Schneeweis, and Branch*
Source and year of publication	*Journal of Management (1990)*
Sample size (number of companies)	131
Sample type	*Fortune Most Admired*
Time of observation	1982-84, 1977-81
Predictors of reputation	alpha, beta, residual error, ROA, debt/asset, income growth, sales growth, operating income growth
Operationalization: how predictors are measured	*Compustat*, CRSP
Outcome variable(s)	reputation
Operationalization: how outcome variable is measured	eight attributes in *Fortune* corporate reputation survey (only results for the one attribute on social responsibility are reported here)
Control variable(s)	industry
Analysis	correlation
General result	+ and 0 and -
Statistical particulars and/or summary of the data analysis	for our purposes, only the *Fortune* attribute for social responsibility (responsibility to the community and environment) is reported; correlations between prior performance and reputation with p<.01: negative for ROA, debt/assets, growth, residuals; positive for alpha (risk); correlations between reputation and subsequent performance with p<.01: negative for debt/assets, residuals; positive for ROA and operating leverage; all other relationships are n.s. and thus counted as zero
Strength of results	moderate
Authors' recommendations for future research	investigate influence of prior firm performance, consider financial performance as a variable influencing social responsibility

137

MISCELLANEOUS:
2 Studies

Investigator(s)	*Buehler and Shetty*
Source and year of publication	*Academy of Management Journal (1976)*
Sample size (number of companies)	232 and 69
Sample type	232 respondents from contacting 1,250 firms on *Fortune's* list of largest U.S. firms; 69 companies in Senator Moss's 1972 report on consumer affairs programs
Time of observation	1969-72
Predictors	size, industry, profitability, ownership
Operationalization: how predictors are measured	NA
Outcome variable(s)	structural changes and programs (five types of activities in each of three areas: urban affairs, consumer affairs, environmental affairs) designed to meet external pressures to adopt CSP activities
Operationalization: how outcome variable is measured	questionnaire and Senate report
Control variable(s)	none
Analysis	F-tests
Result	0: company size, industry, profitability, and ownership (number of stockholders) have some impact on the percentage of companies adopting new CSP programs or structural changes; "However, a large number of the sampled firms, more than one-third, had not effected internal changes. Therefore, despite tremendous public and government pressure, it can be concluded that many firms are apparently not prepared to make well-planned and integrated responses to the corporate responsibility challenge" (p. 77)
Statistical particulars and/or summary of the data analysis	although not an explicit study of the CSP-FP link, the available evidence shows that the impact of profitability on structural changes relevant to CSP is non-significant
Strength of results	weak
Authors' recommendations for future research	NA

Investigator(s)	*Navarro*
Source and year of publication	*Journal of Business (1988)*
Sample size (number of companies)	249
Sample type	*American Council for the Arts (ACA) Guide to Corporate Giving* (mostly *Fortune 1000*)
Time of observation	1976-82
Predictors	(1) profit maximization, (2) managers' utility maximization
Operationalization: how predictors are measured	(1a) advertising (*Compustat*), (1b) labor attraction (*Compustat, ACA Guide*), (1c) free-riding by other companies (*Census of Other Manufactures*), (2a) managerial control (10k, *Million Dollar Directory*), (2b) debt/equity (*Compustat*), (2c) CEO Salary (10k), (2e) Federal income taxes (*Compustat*)
Outcome variable(s)	charitable contributions
Operationalization: how outcome variable is measured	*ACA Guide to Corporate Giving*
Control variable(s)	size (equal response rate) was weighted but concluded it did not matter
Analysis	Regression (OLS, WLS)
Result	(1) +, (2) 0
Statistical particulars and/or summary of the data analysis	(1a) p<.05, (1b) p<.02, (1c) p<.05
Strength of results	strong
Authors' recommendations for future research	estimating the elasticity of substitution between contribution and government expenditures; study the effect of firm size, and collaterally, mergers on contributions

Bibliography

I. Materials Included in the Compendium of 95 Studies

A. Explicit Tests of a Relationship between Corporate Social and Financial Performance

Abbott, Walter F. and R. Joseph Monsen. 1979. On the measurement of corporate social responsibility: Self-reported disclosures as a method of measuring corporate social involvement. *Academy of Management Journal*, 22 (3): 501-515.

Alexander, Gordon J. and Rogene A. Buchholz. 1978. Corporate social responsibility and stock market performance. *Academy of Management Journal*, 21 (3): 479-486.

Anderson, John C. and Alan W. Frankle. 1980. Voluntary social reporting: An iso-beta portfolio analysis. *The Accounting Review,* 55 (3): 467-479.

Aupperle, Kenneth E., Archie B. Carroll, and John D. Hatfield. 1985. An empirical examination of the relationship between corporate social responsibility and profitability. *Academy of Management Journal,* 28 (2): 446-463.

Belkaoui, Ahmed. 1976. The impact of the disclosure of the environmental effects of organizational behavior on the market. *Financial Management,* 5 (4): 26-31.

Berman, Shawn L., Andrew C. Wicks, Suresh Kotha, and Thomas M. Jones. 1999. Does stakeholder orientation matter? The relationship between stakeholder management models and firm financial performance. *Academy of Management Journal*, 42 (5): 488-506.

Blacconiere, Walter G. and W. Dana Northcut. 1997. Environmental information and market reactions to environmental legislation. *Journal of Accounting, Auditing, & Finance*, 12 (2): 149-178.

Blacconiere, Walter G. and Dennis M. Patten. 1994. Environmental disclosures, regulatory costs, and changes in firm value. *Journal of Accounting and Economics*, 18: 357-377.

Bowman, Edward H. 1978. Strategy, annual reports, and alchemy. *California Management Review,* 20 (3): 64-71.

Bowman, Edward H. and Mason Haire. 1975. A strategic posture toward corporate social responsibility. *California Management Review,* 18 (2): 49-58.

Boyle, Edmund J., Mark M. Higgins, and S. Ghon Rhee. 1997. Stock market reaction to ethical initiatives of defense contractors: theory and evidence. *Critical Perspectives on Accounting*, 8: 541-561.

Bragdon, Joseph H., Jr. and John A. T. Marlin. 1972. Is pollution profitable? *Risk Management,* 19 (4): 9-18.

Brown, Brad. 1997. Stock market valuation of reputation for corporate social performance. *Corporate Reputation Review*, 1 (1 & 2): 76-80.

Brown, Brad. 1998. Do stock market investors reward reputation for corporate social performance? *Corporate Reputation Review*, 1 (3): 271-282.

Buehler, Vernon M. and Y. K. Shetty. 1976. Managerial response to social responsibility challenge. *Academy of Management Journal*, 19 (1): 66-78.

Chen, Kung H. and Richard W. Metcalf. 1980. The relationship between pollution control record and financial indicators revisited. *The Accounting Review*, 55 (1): 168-177.

Christmann, Petra. 2000. Effects of "best practices" of environmental management on cost advantage: The role of complementary assets. *Academy of Management Journal*, 43 (4): 663-680.

Clarkson, Max B. E. 1988. Corporate social performance in Canada, 1976-86. In L. E. Preston (Ed.), *Research in Corporate Social Performance and Policy*, vol. 10: 241-265. Greenwich, CT: JAI Press.

Cochran, Phillip L. and Robert A. Wood. 1984. Corporate social responsibility and financial performance. *Academy of Management Journal*, 27 (1): 42-56.

Conine, Thomas E, Jr. and Gerald P. Madden. 1986. Corporate social responsibility and investment value: The expectational relationship. In W. K. Guth (Ed.), *Handbook of Business Strategy: 1986/1987 Yearbook*. Boston, MA: Warren Gorham and Lamont.

Cottrill, Melville T. 1990. Corporate social responsibility and the marketplace. *Journal of Business Ethics*, 9: 723-729.

Diltz, David J. 1995. The private cost of socially responsible investing. *Applied Financial Economics*, 5 (2): 69-77

Dowell, Glen, Stuart Hart, and Bernard Yeung. 1999. Do corporate global environmental standards create or destroy market value? *Management Science*, 46(8): 1059-1074.

Fogler, H. Russell and Fred Nutt. 1975. A note on social responsibility and stock valuation. *Academy of Management Journal*, 18 (1): 155-160.

Freedman, Martin and Bikki Jaggi. 1982. Pollution disclosures, pollution performance and economic performance. *Omega,* 10 (2): 167-176.

Freedman, Martin and Bikki Jaggi. 1986. An analysis of the impact of corporate pollution disclosures included in annual financial statements on investors' decisions. In M. Neimark (Ed.), *Advances in Public Interest Accounting*, 1: 193-212.

Freedman, Martin and A. J. Stagliano. 1991. Differences in social-cost disclosures: A market test of investor reactions. *Accounting, Auditing & Accountability Journal*, 4 (1): 68-83.

Fry, Fred L. and Robert J. Hock. 1976. Who claims corporate responsibility? The biggest and the worst. *Business and Society Review,* 18: 62-65.

Galaskiewicz, Joseph. 1997. An urban grants economy revisited: Corporate charitable contributions in the twin cities, 1979-81, 1987-89. *Administrative Science Quarterly,* 42: 445-471.

Graves, Samuel B. and Sandra A. Waddock. Forthcoming. Beyond built to last . . . Stakeholder relations in "Built-to-Last" Companies. *Business and Society Review.*

Griffin, Jennifer J. and John F. Mahon. 1997. The corporate social performance and corporate financial performance debate: Twenty-five years of incomparable research. *Business & Society,* 36(1): 5-31.

Guerard, John B., Jr. 1997. Is there a cost to being socially responsible in investing? *The Journal of Investing,* Summer, 6 (2): 11-18.

Guerard, John B., Jr. 1997. Additional evidence on the cost of being socially responsible in investing. *The Journal of Investing,* Winter, 6 (4): 31-36.

Hamilton, Sally, Hoje Jo, and Meir Statman. 1993. Doing well while doing good? The investment performance of socially responsible mutual funds. *Financial Analysts Journal,* Nov/Dec: 62-66.

Hart, Stuart L. and Gautam Ahuja. 1996. Does it pay to be green? An empirical examination of the relationship between emission reduction and firm performance. *Business Strategy and the Environment,* 5: 30-37.

Heinze, David C. 1976. Financial correlates of a social involvement measure. *Akron Business and Economic Review,* 7 (1): 48-51.

Herremans, Irene M., Parporn Akathaporn, and Morris McInnes. 1993. An investigation of corporate social responsibility reputation and economic performance. *Accounting, Organizations and Society,* 18 (7/8): 587-604.

Holman, Walter R., J. Randolph New, and Daniel Singer. 1990. The impact of corporate social responsiveness on shareholder wealth. In Lee Preston (Ed.), *Corporation and Society Research: Studies in Theory and Measurement*: 265-280. Greenwich, CT: JAI Press.

Ingram, Robert W. 1978. An investigation of the information content of (certain) social responsibility disclosures. *Journal of Accounting Research,* 16 (2): 270-285.

Ingram, Robert W. and Katherine Beal Frazier. 1983. Narrative disclosures in annual reports. *Journal of Business Research,* 11: 49-60.

Judge, William Q., Jr. and Thomas J. Douglas. 1998. Performance implications of incorporating natural environmental issues into the strategic planning process: An empirical assessment. *Journal of Management Studies,* 35 (2): 241-262.

Kedia, Banwari L. and Edwin C. Kuntz. 1981. The context of social performance: An empirical study of Texas banks. In L.E. Preston (Ed.), *Research in Corporate Social Performance and Policy,* vol. 3: 133-154. Greenwich, CT: JAI Press.

Klassen, Robert D. and Curtis P. McLaughlin. 1996. The impact of environmental management on firm performance. *Management Science,* 42 (8): 1199-1214.

Klassen, Robert D. and D. Clay Whybark. 1999. The impact of environmental technologies on manufacturing performance. *Academy of Management Journal,* 42 (6): 599-615.

Lashgari, Malek K. and David R. Gant. 1989. Social investing: The Sullivan principles. *Review of Social Economy,* 47: 74-83.

Lerner, Linda D. and Gerald D. Fryxell. 1988. An empirical study of the predictors of corporate social performance: A multi-dimensional analysis. *Journal of Business Ethics,* 7: 951-959.

Levy, Ferdinand K. and Gloria M. Shatto. 1980. Social responsibility in large electric utility firms: The case for philanthropy. In L.E. Preston (Ed.), *Research in Corporate Social Performance and Policy,* vol. 2: 237-249. Greenwich, CT: JAI Press, Inc.

Maddox, Katherine E., and John J. Siegfried. 1980. The effect of economic structure on corporate philanthropy. In John J. Siegfried (Ed), *The Economics of Firm Size, Market Structure and Social Performance*: 202-225. Washington, D.C.: Bureau of Economics, Federal Trade Commission.

Marcus, Alfred A., and Robert S. Goodman. 1986. Compliance and performance: Toward a contingency theory. In L.E. Preston and J.E. Post (Eds.), *Research in Corporate Social Performance and Policy,* vol. 8: 193-221. Greenwich, CT: JAI Press.

McGuire, Jean B., Thomas Schneeweis, and Ben Branch. 1990. Perceptions of firm quality: A cause or result of firm performance. *Journal of Management,* 16 (1): 167-180.

McGuire, Jean B., Alison Sundgern, and Thomas Schneeweis. 1988. Corporate social responsibility and firm financial performance. *Academy of Management Journal,* 31 (4): 854-872.

McWilliams, Abagail and Donald Siegel. 2000. Corporate social responsibility and financial performance: Correlation or misspecification? *Strategic Management Journal,* 21: 603-609.

Meznar, Martin B., Douglas Nigh, Chuck C. Y. Kwok. 1994. Effect of announcements of withdrawal from South Africa on stockholder wealth. *Academy of Management Journal,* 37 (6): 1633-1648.

Mills, Dixie L. and Mona J. Gardner. 1984. Financial profiles and the disclosure of expenditures for socially responsible purposes. *Journal of Business Research,* 12 (4): 407-424.

Moskowitz, Milton. 1972. Choosing socially responsible stocks. *Business and Society Review,* 1: 71-75.

Nehrt, Chad. 1996. Timing and intensity effects of environmental investments. *Strategic Management Journal*, 17: 535-547.

Newgren, Kenneth E., Arthur A. Rasher, Margaret E. LaRoe, and Martha R. Szabo. 1985. Environmental assessment and corporate performance: A longitudinal analysis using a market-determined performance measure. In Lee E. Preston (Ed.), *Research in Corporate Social Performance and Policy,* vol. 7: 153-164. Greenwich, CT: JAI Press.

Ogden, Stuart, and Robert Watson. 1999. Corporate Performance and stakeholder management: Balancing shareholder and customer interests in the U.K. privatized water industry. *Academy of Management Journal*, 42 (5): 526-538.

O'Neill, Hugh M., Charles B. Saunders, and Anne Derwinski McCarthy. 1989. Board members, corporate social responsiveness and profitability: Are tradeoffs necessary? *Journal of Business Ethics*, 8: 353-357.

Parket, I. Robert and Henry Eilbert. 1975. Social responsibility: The underlying factors. *Business Horizons,* 18(4): 5-10.

Patten, Dennis M. 1990. The market reaction to social responsibility disclosures: The case of the Sullivan principles signings. *Accounting, Organizations and Society*, 15 (6): 575-587.

Patten, Dennis M. 1991. Exposure, legitimacy, and social disclosure. *Journal of Accounting and Public Policy*, 10: 297-308.

Pava, Moses L. and Joshua Krausz. 1996. The association between corporate social-responsibility and financial performance: The paradox of social cost. *Journal of Business Ethics,* 15: 321-357.

Porter, Michael E. and Class van der Linde. 1995. Green and competitive: Ending the stalemate. *Harvard Business Review*, 73 (5): 120-134.

Posnikoff, Judith F. 1997. Disinvestment from South Africa: They did well by doing good. *Contemporary Economic Policy*, 15 (1): 76-86.

Preston, Lee E. 1978. Analyzing corporate social performance: Methods and results. *Journal of Contemporary Business,* 7: 135-150.

Preston, Lee E. and Douglas P. O'Bannon. 1997. The corporate social-financial performance relationship: A typology and analysis. *Business & Society,* 36 (4): 419-429.

Preston, Lee E. and Harry J. Sapienza. 1990. Stakeholder management and corporate performance. *Journal of Behavioral Economics,* 19 (4): 361-375.

Roberts, Robin W. 1992. Determinants of corporate social responsibility disclosure: An application of stakeholder theory. *Accounting, Organizations and Society,* 17 (6): 595-612.

Rockness, Joanne, Paul Schlachter, and Howard O. Rockness. 1986. Hazardous waste disposal, corporate disclosure and financial performance in the chemical industry. *Advances in Public Interest Accounting,* 1: 167-191.

Russo, Michael V. and Paul A. Fouts. 1997. A resource-based perspective on corporate environmental performance and profitability. *Academy of Management Journal,* 40 (3): 534-559.

Shane, Philip B. and Barry H. Spicer. 1983. Market response to environmental information produced outside the firm. *The Accounting Review,* 58 (3): 521-538.

Sharma, Sanjay and Harrie Vredenburg. 1998. Proactive corporate environmental strategy and the development of competitively valuable organizational capabilities. *Strategic Management Journal,* 19: 729-753.

Spencer, Barbara A. and G. Stephen Taylor. 1987. A within and between analysis of the relationship between corporate social responsibility and financial performance. *Akron Business and Economic Review,* 18 (3): 7-18.

Spicer, Barry H. 1978. Investors, corporate social performance, and information disclosure: An empirical study. *The Accounting Review,* 53: 94-111.

Stevens, William P. 1984. Market reaction to corporate environmental performance. *Advances in Accounting,* 1: 41-61.

Sturdivant, Frederick D. and James L. Ginter. 1977. Corporate social responsiveness: Management attitudes and economic performance. *California Management review,* 19 (3): 30-39.

Teoh, Siew Hong, Ivo Welch, and C. Paul Wazzan. 1999. The effect of socially activist investment policies on the financial markets: Evidence from the South African boycott. *Journal of Business,* 72 (1): 35-89.

Tichy, Noel M., Andrew R. McGill, and Lynda St. Clair. 1997. Introduction: Corporate global citizenship – why now? In Noel M. Tichy, Andrew R. McGill, and Lynda St. Clair (Eds.), *Corporate Global Citizenship: Doing Business in the Public Eye*: 1-22. San Francisco: The New Lexington Press.

Vance, Stanley C. 1975. Are socially responsible corporations good investment risks? *Management Review,* 64: 18-24.

Verschoor, Curtis C. 1998. A study of the link between a corporation's financial performance and its commitment to ethics. *Journal of Business Ethics,* 17: 1509-1516.

Waddock, Sandra A. and Samuel B. Graves. 1997. The corporate social performance-financial performance link. *Strategic Management Journal*, 18 (4): 303-319.

Waddock, Sandra A., Samuel B. Graves, and Renee Gorski. 2000. Performance characteristics of social and traditional investments. *Journal of Investing*, 9 (2): 27–38.

Wokutch, Richard E. and Barbara A. Spencer. 1987. Corporate saints and sinners: The effects of philanthropic and illegal activity on organizational performance. *California Management Review*, 29 (2): 62-77.

Wright, Peter and Stephen P. Ferris. 1997. Agency conflict and corporate strategy: The effect of divestment on corporate value. *Strategic Management Journal*, 18: 77-83.

B. Available Evidence on the Relationship between Corporate Social and Financial Performance[1]

Belkaoui, Ahmed and Philip G. Karpik. 1989. Determinants of the corporate decision to disclose social information. *Accounting, Auditing, and Accountability Journal*, 2 (1): 36-51.

Brown, Brad and Susan Perry. 1994. Removing the financial performance halo from Fortune's "most admired" companies. *Academy of Management Journal*, 37 (5): 1347-59.

Cowen, Scott S., Linda B. Ferreri, and Lee D. Parker. 1987. The impact of corporate characteristics on social responsibility disclosure: A typology and frequency-based analysis. *Accounting, Organizations and Society*, 12 (2): 111-222.

Fombrun, Charles and Mark Shanley. 1990. What's in a name? Reputation building and corporate strategy. *Academy of Management Journal*, 33 (2): 233-258.

Fry, Louis W., Gerald D. Keim, and Roger E. Meiners. 1982. Corporate contributions: Altruistic or for profit? *Academy of Management Journal*, 25: 94-106.

Graves, Samuel B. and Sandra A. Waddock. 1994. Institutional owners and corporate social performance. *Academy of Management Journal*, 37: 1034-1046.

Johnson, Richard A. and Daniel W. Greening. 1999. The effects of corporate governance and institutional ownership types on corporate social performance. *Academy of Management Journal*, 42 (5): 564-576.

Navarro, Peter. 1988. Why do corporations give to charity? *Journal of Business*, 61 (1): 65-93.

Simerly, Roy L. 1995. The institutional ownership, corporate social performance, and firms' financial performance. *Psychological Reports*, 77: 515-525.

---

[1] Although these references include data about the relationship between corporate social and financial performance, the authors do not focus on testing that relationship, and the data appear as part of investigations into other research questions.

II. Reviews of the Literature on Corporate Social and Financial Performance

Aldag, Ramon J. and Kathryn M. Bartol. 1978. Empirical studies of corporate social performance and policy: A survey of problems and results. *Research in Corporate Social Performance and Policy*, 1: 165-199.

Arlow, Peter and Martin J. Gannon. 1982. Social responsiveness, corporate structure, and economic performance. *Academy of Management Review*, 7 (2): 235-241.

Aupperle, Kenneth E., Archie B. Carroll, and John D. Hatfield. 1985. An empirical examination of the relationship between corporate social responsibility and profitability. *Academy of Management Journal,* 28 (2): 446-463.

Cochran, Phillip L. and Robert A. Wood. 1984. Corporate social responsibility and financial performance. *Academy of Management Journal,* 27 (1): 42-56.

Griffin, Jennifer J. and John F. Mahon. 1997. The corporate social performance and corporate financial performance debate: Twenty-five years of incomparable research. *Business & Society,* 36(1): 5-31.

Pava, Moses L. and Joshua Krausz. 1996. The association between corporate social-responsibility and financial performance: The paradox of social cost. *Journal of Business Ethics,* 15: 321-357.

Preston, Lee E. and Douglas P. O'Bannon. 1997. The corporate social-financial performance relationship: A typology and analysis. *Business & Society,* 36 (4): 419-429.

Richardson, Alan J., Michael Welker, and Ian R. Hutchinson. 1999. Managing capital market reactions to corporate social responsibility. *International Journal of Management Reviews*, 1 (1): 17-43.

Roman, Ronald M., Sefa Hayibor, Bradley R. Agle. 1999. The relationship between social and financial performance. *Business & Society*, 38 (1): 109-125.

Ullmann, Arieh A. 1985. Data in search of a theory: A critical examination of the relationships among social performance, social disclosure, and economic performance of U.S. firms. *Academy of Management Review*, 10 (3): 540-557.

Wokutch, Richard E. and Elizabeth W. McKinney. 1991. Behavioral and perceptual measures of corporate social performance. In James E. Post (Ed.), *Research in Corporate Social Performance and Policy*, 12: 309-330.

Wood, Donna J. and Raymond E. Jones. 1995. Stakeholder mismatching: A theoretical problem in empirical research on corporate social performance. *The International Journal of Organizational Analysis*, 3 (3): 229-267.

III. Methodological Critiques

Fryxell, Gerald E. and Jia Wang. 1994. The Fortune corporate 'reputation' index: Reputation for what? *Journal of Management,* 20 (1): 1-14.

Gephart, Robert P., Jr. 1991. Multiple methods for tracking corporate social performance: Insights from a study of major industrial accidents. In James E. Post (Ed.), *Research in Corporate Social Performance and Policy*, vol. 12: 359-383. Greenwich, CT: JAI Press.

McWilliams, Abagail and Donald Siegel. 1997. Event studies in management research: Theoretical and empirical issues. *Academy of Management Journal*, 40 (3): 626-657.

McWilliams, Abagail, Donald Siegel, and Siew Hong Teoh. 1999. Issues in the use of the event study methodology: A critical analysis of corporate social responsibility studies. *Organizational Research Methods*, 2 (4): 350-372.

Ruf, Bernadette M., Krishnamurty Muralidhar, and Karen Paul. 1998. The development of a systematic, aggregate measure of corporate social performance. *Journal of Management*, 24 (1): 119-133.

Simerly, Roy L. 1999. Measuring corporate social performance: An assessment of techniques. *International Journal of Management*, 16 (2): 253-257.

Spicer, Barry H. 1978. Accounting for corporate social performance: Some problems and issues. *Journal of Contemporary Business*, 7 (Winter): 151-170.

Wokutch, Richard E. and Elizabeth W. McKinney. 1991. Behavioral and perceptual measures of corporate social performance. In James E. Post (Ed.), *Research in Corporate Social Performance and Policy*, vol. 12: 309-330.

IV. Theoretical Background

Angel, James J. and Pietra Rivoli. 1997. Does ethical investing impose a cost upon the firm? A theoretical perspective. *The Journal of Investing*, 6 (4): 57-61.

Berle, Adolph A., Jr. 1931. Corporate powers as powers in trust. *Harvard Law Review*, 44 (7): 1049-1074.

Bradley, Michael, Cindy A. Schipani, Anant K. Sundaram, and James P. Walsh. 1999. The purposes and accountability of the corporation in contemporary society: Corporate governance at a crossroads. *Law and Contemporary Problems*, 62 (3): 9-86

Carroll, Archie B. 1979. A three-dimensional conceptual model of corporate social performance. *Academy of Management Review,* 4 (4): 497-505.

Clarkson, Max B. E. 1995. A stakeholder framework for analyzing and evaluating corporate social performance. *Academy of Management Review*, 20 (1): 92-117.

Davis, Keith. 1973. The case for and against business assumption of social responsibilities. *Academy of Management Journal*, 16 (2): 312-322.

Dodd, E. Merrick, Jr. 1932. For whom are corporate managers trustees? *Harvard Law Review*, 45 (7): 1145-1163.

Donaldson, Thomas and Thomas W. Dunfee. 1999. *Ties that bind: a social contracts approach to business ethics*. Boston: Harvard Business School Press.

Donaldson, Thomas and Lee E. Preston. 1995. The stakeholder theory of the corporation: Concepts, evidence, and implications. *Academy of Management Review*, 20 (1): 65-91

Freeman, R. Edward 1984. *Strategic Management: A Stakeholder Approach*. Boston: Pitman/Ballinger.

Friedman, Milton. 1970. The social responsibility of business is to increase its profits. *New York Times Magazine*, September 13: 32-33, 122-126.

Hay, Robert and Ed Gray. 1974. Social responsibilities of business managers. *Academy of Management Journal*, 17 (1): 135-143.

Jones, Thomas M. 1995. Instrumental stakeholder theory: A synthesis of ethics and economics. *Academy of Management Review*, 20 (2):404-437.

Keim, Gerald D. 1978. Corporate social responsibility: An assessment of the enlightened self-interest model. *Academy of Management Review*, 3 (1):32-39.

Kochan, Thomas A. and Saul A. Rubinstein 2000. Toward a stakeholder theory of the firm: The Saturn partnership. *Organization Science* 11 (4): 367-386

Levitt, Theodore 1958. The dangers of social responsibility. *Harvard Business Review*, 36 (5): 41-50.

Orts, Eric W. 1993. The complexity and legitimacy of corporate law. *Washington and Lee Law Review*, 50 (4): 1565-1623.

Sethi, S. Prakash 1979. A conceptual framework for environmental analysis of social issues and evaluation of business response patterns. *Academy of Management Review*, 4 (1): 63-74.

Swanson, Diane L. 1995. Addressing a theoretical problem by reorienting the corporate social performance model. *Academy of Management Review*, 20 (1): 43-64.

Wartick, Steven L. and Philip L. Cochran 1985. The evolution of the corporate social performance model. *Academy of Management Review*, 10 (4): 758-769.

Wood, Donna J. 1991. Corporate social performance revisited. *Academy of Management Review*, 16 (4): 691-718.

Wood, Donna J. 1991. Social issues in management: Research and theory in corporate social performance. *Journal of Management*, 17: 383-406.

V. Additional Materials Referred to in the Book

Austin, James E. 1998. The invisible side of leadership. *Leader to Leader*, Spring 1998: 38-46.

Brown, Brad and Susan Perry. 1995. Some additional thoughts on halo-removed Fortune residuals. *Business & Society*, 34 (2): 236-240.

Capon, Noel, John U. Farley, and Scott Hoenig. 1990. Determinants of financial performance: A meta-analysis. *Management Science*, 36 (10): 1143-1159.

Frooman, Jeff. 1997. Socially irresponsible and illegal behavior and shareholder wealth: A meta-analysis of event studies. *Business & Society*, 36 (3): 221-249.

Jaffe, Adam B., Steven R. Peterson, Paul R. Portney, and Robert N. Stavins. 1995. Environmental regulation and the competitiveness of U.S. Manufacturing: What does the evidence tell us? *Journal of Economic Literature*, 33 (March 1995): 132-163.

Margolis, Joshua D. and James P. Walsh. 2000. Misery loves companies: Whither social initiatives by business? University of Michigan Business School Working Paper. Ann Arbor, MI.

Narver, John C. 1971. Rational management responses to external effects. *Academy of Management Journal*, 14: 99-114.

Spicer, Barry H. 1978. Market risk, accounting data, and companies' pollution control records. *Journal of Business Finance and Accounting*, 5 (1): 67-83.

Szwajkowski, Eugene and Raymond E Figlewicz, 1997. Of babies and bathwater. *Business & Society*, 36 (4): 362-286.

Teoh, Hai Yap and Godwin Y. Shiu. 1990. Attitudes towards corporate social responsibility and perceived importance of social responsibility information characteristics in a decision context. *Journal of Business Ethics,* 9: 71-77.

Tetlock, Philip E. 2000. Cognitive biases and organizational correctives: Do both disease and cure depend on the politics of the beholder? *Administrative Science Quarterly*, 45 (2): 293-326.

VI. Related References[2]

Bhambri, Arvind and Jeffrey Sonnenfeld. 1988. Organization structure and corporate social performance: A field study in two contrasting industries. *Academy of Management Journal*, 31 (3): 642-662.

Brown, Brad and Susan Perry. 1995. Halo-removed residuals of Fortune's "Responsibility to the community and environment" – a decade of data. *Business & Society*, 34 (2): 199-215.

Brown, Brad and Susan Perry. 1995. Some additional thoughts on halo-removed Fortune residuals. *Business & Society*, 34 (2): 236-240.

Buzby, Stephen L. and Haim Falk. 1978. A survey of the interest in social responsibility information by mutual funds. *Accounting, Organizations and Society*, 3 (3/4): 191-201.

Buzby, Stephen L. and Haim Falk. 1979. Demand for social responsibility information by university investors. *The Accounting Review*, 54 (1): 23-37.

Chakravarthy, Balaji S. 1986. Measuring strategic performance. *Strategic Management Journal*, 7: 437-458.

Coffey, Betty S. and Gerald E. Fryxell. 1991. Institutional ownership of stock and dimensions of corporate social performance: An empirical examination. *Journal of Business Ethics*, 10: 437-444.

Grossman, Blake R. and William F. Sharpe. 1986. Financial implications of South African Divestment. *Financial Analysts Journal*, July/August: 15-29.

Holmes, Sandra L. 1976. Executive perceptions of corporate social responsibility. *Business Horizons*, 19 (3): 34-40.

Holmes, Sandra L. 1977. Corporate social performance: Past and present areas of commitment. *Academy of Management Journal*, 20 (3): 433-438.

Ingram, Robert W. and Katherine Beal Frazier. 1980. Environmental performance and corporate disclosure. *Journal of Accounting Research*, 18 (2): 614-622.

Keim, Gerald D. 1978. Managerial behavior and the social responsibility debate: Goals versus constraints. *Academy of Management Journal*, 21 (1): 57-68.

Kurtz, Lloyd. 1997. No effect or no *net* effect? Studies on socially responsible investing. *The Journal of Investing*, 6 (4): 37-49.

---

[2] These materials were read for possible inclusion in the compendium of studies investigating a link between social and financial performance. Although they did not meet the specified criteria for inclusion in the compendium, they do inform larger debates about corporate social performance.

Moskowitz, Milton. 1975. Profiles in corporate responsibility: The ten worst, the ten best. *Business and Society Review,* 13: 28-42.

Narver, John C. 1971. Rational management responses to external effects. *Academy of Management Journal*, 14: 99-114.

Reed, Lyman, Kathleen Getz, Denis Collins, William Oberman, and Robert Toy. 1990. Theoretical models and empirical results: A review and synthesis of JAI volumes 1-10. In Lee Preston (Ed.), *Corporation and Society Research: Studies in Theory and Measurement*: 27-62. Greenwich, CT: JAI Press.

Reinhardt, Forest L. 2000. *Down to Earth*. Boston: Harvard Business School Press.

Riahi-Belkaoui, Ahmed. 1992. Executive compensation, organizational effectiveness, social performance and firm performance: An empirical investigation. *Journal of Business Finance and Accounting,* 19 (1): 25-38.

Rudd, Andrew. 1979. Divestment of South African equities: How risky? *The Journal of Portfolio Management*, 5 (3): 5-10.

Rudd, Andrew. 1981. Social responsibility and portfolio performance. *California Management Review*, 23 (4): 55-61.

Sonnenfeld, Jeffrey. 1981. Executive apologies for price fixing: Role biased perceptions of causality. *Academy of Management Journal*, 24 (1): 192-198.

Teoh, Hai-Yap and Gregory Thong. 1984. Another look at corporate social responsibility and reporting: An empirical study in a developing country. *Accounting, Organizations and Society*, 9 (2): 189-206.

Trotman, Ken T. and Graham W. Bradley. 1981. Associations between social responsibility disclosure and characteristics of companies. *Accounting, Organizations and Society,* 6 (4): 355-362.

Verrecchia, Robert E. 1983. Discretionary disclosure. *Journal of Accounting and Economics*, 5: 179-194.

Wiseman, Joanne. 1982. An evaluation of environmental disclosures made in corporate annual reports. *Accounting, Organizations and Society*, 7 (1): 53-63.

Wright, Peter, Stephen P. Ferris, Janine S. Hiller, and Mark Kroll. 1995. Competitiveness through management of diversity: Effects on stock price valuation. *Academy of Management Journal*, 38 (1): 272-287.

Appendix: A Guide to Abbreviations and Acronyms

General Acronyms:

CSP:	corporate social performance
CSR:	corporate social responsibility
FP:	financial performance
NA:	not available
OB:	organizational behavior
OT:	organizational theory
QWL:	quality of work life

Data Source Acronyms:

CEP:	Council on Economic Priorities
CRSP:	Center for Research in Security Prices
KLD:	Kinder, Lydenberg, Domini

Statistical Acronyms:

ANOVA:	analysis of variance
n.s.:	non-significant
OLS:	ordinary least squares
WLS:	weighted least squares

Financial Acronyms:

CAR:	cumulative abnormal returns
EPS:	earnings per share
ROA:	return on assets
ROE:	return on equity
ROI:	return on investment
ROS:	return on sales